THE LAST BIG-GUN NAVAL BATTLE
THE BATTLE OF SURIGAO STRAIT

THE LAST BIG-GUN
NAVAL BATTLE
THE BATTLE OF
SURIGAO STRAIT

AN EYEWITNESS ACCOUNT
HOWARD SAUER
ABOARD USS MARYLAND

THE GLENCANNON PRESS
MARITIME BOOKS

PALO ALTO
1999

Art Director: S.L. Hecht

Copyright © 1999 by Howard Sauer
Published by The Glencannon Press
P.O. Box 341, Palo Alto, CA 94302
Tel. 800-711-8985
www.glencannon.com

First Edition, first printing.

Library of Congress Cataloging-in-Publication Data

Sauer, Howard, 1918-
   The last big-gun- naval battle : the Battle of Surigao Strait /
Howard Sauer. -- 1st ed.
      p.   cm.
   Includes bibliographical references and index.
   ISBN 1-889901-08-3 (hc.)
      1. Sauer, Howard, 1918-   . 2. Philippine Sea, Battles of the, 1944.
3. World War, 1939-1945--Personal narratives, American. 5. United
States. Navy Biography.   6. Sailors--United States Biography.
I. Title
D774.P5S28   1999
940.54'5973--dc21   99-21242
                                                              CIP

DEDICATION

To the officers and men of
USS *Maryland*
killed in action during World War II

These shipmates gave their lives in action with the enemy:

Harold Paul Alcock, BM2c, USNR
Rex William Andrews, GM3c, USNR
Claire R. Brier, MM2c, USN
Freddie Ray Bone, S1c, USNR
Luis Zamora Cedillo, S1c, USNR
"C.H." Chambers, S2c, USNR
"J.A." Conwill, S2c, USNR
Kenneth Cripes, Mus2c, USNR
Howard A. Crow, Ens., USNR
Robert Andrew Dunn, SK3c, USN
Charles Eugene Evans, CTC(T), USN
Eugene Webster Gates, S1c, USN
James B. Ginn, Lt. (jg), USN
James Willis Gist, S1c, USNR
Morris Goldstein, S1c, USN
Roy Petty Hargrove, Jr., S1c, USNR
James Dreadman Harrington, S2c, USNR
William Marion Hathcox, HA1c, USNR
Lawrence Loman Hill, S1c, USNR
Carl Clifford Hilton, F2c, USNR
Charles John Hofmann, F1c, USNR
Leroy Arnold Johnson, Y2c, USN
Stonewall Jackson Kendrick, Jr., S2c, USN
Robert Eugene Kester, HA2c, USNR
Thomas Edward Kukan, S2c, USNR
Fargust Earl Lamb, HA2c, USNR

Harold McClellan Lanning, S2c, USNR
Arnold Leon Land, S1c, USNR
Leslie Gerald Longford, S2c, USNR
Jack Stephen Lucas, S1c, USNR
Carroll F. Lutz, S1c, USN
Jack Edward Mangold, F1c, USNR
Pete Clovis Manly, HA2c, USNR
Robert Travis Markshausen, FC3c, USNR
Warren H. McCutcheon, S2c, USNR
Jack Edward Medaris, S1c, USNR
Lloyd Thomas Milligan, S1c, USNR
Victor Day Newman, SF2c, USNR
Rudolph Raymond Niss, EM1c, USNR
William Orville Noel, COX, USN
Irwin George Nopen, GM3c, USN
Henry Joseph O'Rourke, S1c, USNR
Rufus Miller Overstreet, Jr., S2c, USNR
"J.R." Peacock, S1c, USNR
Laten Francis Riley, BM1c, USN
Gordon Odell Ryman, S1c, USNR
Harold Aric Scott, Cox., USN
Edward Herbert Seagraves, GM2c, USNR
Raymond William Sturgeon, S1c, USN
Melvin Thau, S1c, USN
Glen Carmack Thomas, S2c, USNR
Hollice Lloyd Voyles, Y2c, USN
Clyde Tennyson White, BM2c, USN
Vernon Ray Williams, HA1c, USNR
Robert Murray Wooldridge, S1c, USNR
Vernon Zoller, CBM, USN

ACKNOWLEDGEMENTS

The professional assistance of the following people
and organizations were a great help in creating this work:

Professor Kanji Akagi, Military History Department,
The National Institute for Defense Studies, Japan.
Robert Campbell, translator, University of California,
Berkeley.
Bernard F. Cavalcante, Head, Operational Archives
Branch, Naval Historical Center, Washington Navy
Yard.
Danny J. Crawford, Head, Reference Section, History
and Museums Division, Headquarters, U. S. Marine
Corps.
Dan A. Godeke, attorney-at-law, Fort Bragg.
Captain Shin Itonaga, JMSDF (Ret.)

Stanley Kalkus, Director, Navy Department Library, Naval Historical Center, Washington Navy Yard.

Richard C. Lina, Appraiser, Estates Gallery, Fort Bragg.

R.H. Pelvin, Naval Historical Officer, Australian Navy

John C. Reilly, Jr., Ships' Histories Section, Naval Historical Center, Washington Navy Yard.

Mrs. Janet Siebert, retired editor, University of California Press.

Commander Paul Stillwell, USN (Ret.), United States Naval Institute, Annapolis.

I would also like to thank the following for their contributions: Robert O. Baumrucker, Firman J. Balza, Justin J. David, Freeman A. Flynn, Ph.D., Maurice Fraga, E. Wilbur Fredell, M.D., Fleet A. Hamby, Robert C. Houle, H. Corwin Johnson, Alfred Merrill, Clyde Moslander, Wayne Ring, James G. Rizer, Hunter S. Robbins, Jr., Paul and Mary Sauer, Leslie Short, Michael Spies and Russell Terrill.

And, finally, those who helped by simply encouraging me, perhaps the greatest contribution of all: Ms. Karin Asmussen, John Bailey, Jack Carlson, Mrs. Bethena Cooney, Dick Beaman, President, USS *Maryland* BB-46 Veterans Association, Ms. Peggy Fairfield, Mrs. Alberta Foster, George F. Gruner, David Gurney, Mrs. Lorraine Henderson, Thomas J. Heston, Professor of History, West Chester University, Dean L. Mawdsley, M.D., Mrs. Velma Patterson, Roger Phillips, Raymond J. Pivirotto, Douglas Roycroft, Mrs. Helen Stauer, Mrs. Helen Thompson, Fred R. Wellner and Mrs. Sally Zalkus.

Also, many thanks to Capt. Walter Jaffee, editorial director of The Glencannon Press, for his most welcome editorial assistance.

Contents

AUTHOR'S FOREWORD

This is an opportunity to record my honest belief that Captain Wilson and the other captains under whom we served on *Maryland* and *Colorado* exemplified all that is fine in American manhood.

Their conduct under stress was cool and calm. Their judgment was sound. From the bridge, from sky control just above, or from the foretop way above, never once did we observe shouting or violent gesticulating, nor were we ever subjected to a hasty series of orders and counter orders. And they were all enjoyable company at parties or in occasional conversation during the dark watches on the bridge. Our skippers performed in accordance with their personal codes, not for the approval of a once-young officer who might dare to comment forty and more years later!

However the Navy managed it with the limited funds provided for salaries, for training, and for simple underway time, it seemed to me there existed some marvelous battleship captains ready for wartime service. Without their splendid qualities, *Maryland* — and all the other ships — could not have done what we did in the manner we did it.

So . . .

Captain W. L. Friedell, USN (Commanding officer, USS *Colorado*, 1937)

Captain D. C. Godwin, USN (Also commanding officer, NROTC, University of California, Berkeley)

Captain C. H. Jones, USN

Captain H. J. Ray, USN

Captain J. D. Wilson, USN

Captain B. W. Becker, USN

Yours is a great tradition that goes back to Captain John Paul Jones and goes forward to the future.

Many aspire to the command of a major man-of-war; just a few make it. It requires the best in men, and I've always felt you all had that, and more.

We — all the young men, now older — salute you, gentlemen, and your wives.

PROLOGUE

October 25, 1944.
Surigao Strait, Leyte Gulf, Philippine Islands.

USS *Maryland's* eight monster 16-inch guns were trained to starboard, their barrels elevated. They maintained their alignment with precision as the ship slowly rolled beneath them.

"Commence firing! Commence firing!"

In the darkness ahead, *West Virginia's* main battery flamed and roared about every forty seconds, the red tracers soaring skyward in long curving trajectories then slowly descending into a fountain of shell splashes. The scene was lighted by frequent topside hits on the Japanese battleship, *Yamashiro*.

Now was the moment for which the officers and men on board USS *Maryland* (BB-46) had prepared since she was hit by two bombs during Japan's surprise attack on December 7, 1941 sinking her bow into the mud of Pearl Harbor.

Finally, three years later, retribution was at hand.

Maryland had been repaired, but not completely modernized. Our gun fire control system was not as up-to-date as that of many of the other ships. *West Virginia, California* and *Tennessee* were firing at a great rate, but *Maryland* was painfully silent. With our older Mark 3 fire control radar we couldn't develop a good firing solution. The minutes slid away.

There was only one thought in the minds of all in secondary forward, and of every person on board, as we strained to see the battle:

"We've got to shoot! We've just *got* to shoot!"

1

USS *MARYLAND* (BB-46)

USS *Maryland*'s combat career began on December 7, 1941, but she had a long history before that fateful day. Planning for a new ship (BB-46) for the Battle Line of the United States commenced before 1916, when building funds were allotted. BB-46 was commissioned in 1921. Training for my small role in the last big-gun naval battle began in 1936, my first year in college.

An important benefit of the Navy's University of California at Berkeley Reserve Training Program was the summer cruise on a Pacific Fleet battleship. In 1937, ninety-six of us embarked in USS *Colorado* (BB-45), a battleship with a 16-inch 45-caliber main battery and 5-inch 51-caliber secondary battery.

Assigned to *Colorado*'s port casemates housing the 5-inchers, we literally lived with the guns. Our hammocks and cots were strung over and around and under the gun breeches. We helped with gun maintenance, trained on these guns, fired them in a Short Range Battle Practice. Those broadsiders became a part of our lives, and, to many, they still are.

We received more than the usual training on that 1937 cruise. While we were in Hawaii, Amelia Earhart and her navigator, Fred Noonan, were reported missing on the New Guinea-Howland Island leg of their around-the-world flight. *Colorado* was ordered south to act as head-quarters ship in the search until relieved by the aircraft carrier *Lexington*. We assisted the deck force in the underway refueling of our destroyers and the Coast Guard cutter *Itasca*, observed our aircrafts' dawn-to-dusk flight operations, and stood many foretop lookout watches.

The prewar Naval Reserve Officers' Training Program was special as it was offered at only six American universities. Membership in the NROTC was greatly valued. The instructors were highly qualified regular naval officers and chief petty officers.

Courses in gunnery, navigation, engineering, seamanship, tactics and naval history were well-organized and taught and morale was high.

After a year away from school, I returned and more or less concentrated on those naval courses. Orders to combat ships arrived well before graduation. On May 13, 1942, we were awarded our academic degrees, plus naval reserve ensigns' commissions. Naval Reserve Officers Training Corps classmates Robert Sproul, Jr., Robert Yelland and I were ordered aboard USS *Maryland* (BB-46) for duty.

Our orders allowed a short delay, which I spent with family and friends. Then there was a farewell in Berkeley, a forty-two cent Key System train ride over the new San Francisco Bay Bridge from Berkeley to San Francisco, faithfully paid by the Navy, a taxi to Pier 29, a walk

USS Maryland *as she appeared in February, 1942.   Note aircraft catapult on top of turret No. 3.   U.S. Navy*

down the dock, and I was on board *Maryland*, May 19, 1942 all within six days! I had two thoughts: it was great to feel needed and when do we get underway?

While passing the ship's fine bow on my way to the brow, I noted how it reached far forward, then curved gracefully aft to the waterline.   She was hollow below with an entry resembling that of a clipper ship. (From aloft she was in no way a clipper, giving an impression of power rather than speed.)

A new feature was the five-foot shelf extending fore and aft from amidships and reaching about half way up the sides.   These were the 1941 blisters — added torpedo protection and more fuel capacity which would be useful in the broad reaches of the Pacific.

Over me towered the two cage masts shouldering their way through the fog.   Each carried identical small houses, the fore and main tops, named after the fighting tops of sailing ship days.

The offensive armament of a battleship then was the main gun battery. We had no missiles like those in the Navy's last battleships. *Maryland* possessed, as did *West Virginia* and *Colorado*, eight 16-inch 45-caliber rifles housed two to a turret.   That is, the bore was sixteen inches, and the length was sixteen times forty-five, seven hundred and twenty inches, or sixty feet, not including the powder chamber and breech. The turrets, two forward and two aft, were protected with armor up to eighteen inches thick.

My salutes to the ensign and quarterdeck were proper — traditions which have come down through the years as demonstrations of obeisance to the crucifix once carried on board Christian vessels, and of loyalty. The officer of the deck, in charge of the ship under the captain and executive officer, glanced at me long enough to return my second salute.

"Ensign Sauer reporting for duty, Sir!"

This was a landmark in any young officer's life. We were only beginners. There was a tremendous amount to learn but we were no longer merely students. We had earned a place in the real world.

My feelings were confirmed.

"Very well, *Mister* Sauer, stand by for a sec, *please.*"

Aboard ship, by custom, everyone tolerates the unsure, untried, new officer. His responsibilities are minimal then, only his rank is respected.

It was a busy scene that May day on the quarterdeck. There seemed to be an unusual number of quite senior officers hastily arriving and departing.

Maryland was then one of the newest battleships on active duty in the Pacific, the flagship of Rear Admiral W.S. Anderson, COMBATPAC (COMmander, BATtleships, PACific). An admiral with an operational and/or administrative command usually had a staff consisting of a chief of staff and officers concerned with operations, gunnery, communications, aviation, engineering, logistics, and other functions. The more ships under the admiral's command, the more work and the more assistants.

A tap on my shoulder interrupted my study of the smaller guns. "Welcome aboard!" There stood Ensign

USS Maryland *in the New Hebrides in 1943. Stations from the top down: radar antenna, main battery spot 1, secondary forward (broadside battery control station), sky control (5-inch antiaircraft directors, sky lookouts, stereo rangefinder), navigation bridge (conning tower) and flag bridge (signalmen). U.S. Navy.*

W.G. Flynn, USNR,[1] an engineering junior officer. We talked for a moment, but still keyed up, I went back to the brow to check my personal gear. It was missing!

---

[1] Throughout the text Navy personnel are indicated as USN or USNR. USN indicates regular Navy or someone intending to make a career of that branch of the service. USNR refers to those who have joined because of a need for additional personnel created by a national emergency (World War II in this case).

Mr. Flynn reassured me: "You'll probably find it in the JOBR (Junior Officers' Bunk Room) where you'll stay for a while."

There was a brief tour of the ship, coffee in the junior officers' mess, where I met several of my new shipmates, and then Ensign Flynn led me to my bunk.

My first day on board was long. After stowing my gear in the locker assigned and testing my new bunk for comfort, I moved again to the junior officers' mess. It was our clubhouse, actually. We not only ate there, we lived there when we were not on watch, working, or studying. We also used the space to entertain guests.

In the mess that evening were many more of my newly acquired shipmates: Bill Luce, always laughing, kidding; big Frank Springer, whom I came to know well as my division officer; Rex Raleigh, antiaircraft wizard; Bill Witherspoon, Bill Robertson, an attorney in civilian life; Carl Olson, U.S. Naval Academy, Class of 1942, and others. The ship's roster of officers, dated June 1, 1942, lists forty-nine ensigns and a second lieutenant from the Marine Corps, L. N. Casey.

It was impossible to know then what they all did aboard *Maryland*, but I was confident I would in time learn the various slots and who was assigned where. They were friendly in a casual way, and soon I began to experience the feeling of membership in a club.

Shipboard life can be enjoyable, if there is a good group aboard. Perhaps it isn't the individuals; assignment of the junior officers and most of the ratings is by letter or dispatch. There are no personal interviews as there would be in a business firm. Except in the submarine service, I knew of no personality tests. There could be other reasons for the friendly, usually happy spirit that permeated the hundreds of passageways and compartments which made up the interior of the old ship. I have since talked to many officers and men who served aboard her, who passed time in other ships, and so have a basis for comparison. Most agree: "*Maryland* was always a happy ship!"

Dinner that first evening aboard stands out because of all the kidding that went on while we ate.

Ensign C.A. McGowan, USN, a junior division officer in Turret II of the main battery, was the first target. It was then we new officers heard the dive bomber story.

From somewhere in the messroom came the sound of a dive bomber. Those Pearl Harbor veterans could do it just right. Ensign McGowan's face turned red. Laughter. A little later from a corner came a shout: "Dive bomber!" Red face again.

The explanation was that Ensign McGowan reported aboard from the Naval Academy just after the ship arrived in Bremerton, Washington, for repair following the attack at Pearl Harbor. At Pearl Harbor one bomb hit and exploded on the forecastle, spraying the tops with fragments. The second landed close aboard, pierced the ship's side, exploded, and flooded several compartments. The bow sank into the mud.

From then on the gunnery department took no chances. Twenty-four hour watches were stood on the antiaircraft guns, even in the States. Mac was immediately stationed on watch as a boat deck 5-inch AA battery officer. On his first watch Admiral Anderson happened past.

To test the efficiency of the ship's antiaircraft protection, the admiral pointed skyward and shouted: "Dive bombers!"

Ensign McGowan frantically scanned the murky night sky.

No enemy . . .

His four gun crews also searched.

Nothing . . .

The seconds seemed like minutes as COMBATPAC peered skyward. What to do?

"I can't tell the admiral he's mistaken; neither can I shoot with nothing at which to shoot!"

Mac was on the point of letting one go for the sound effects, when the admiral saved the day by calling: "Simulate!"

This was an order familiar in those days of intensive drill. The gun crews went through the routine of preparing the guns for firing while Mac gasped with relief. To have another Pearl Harbor on one's first day aboard is not something to be taken lightly. But to label this incident as improbable, or to dismiss the young officer's genuine concern as unlikely, is not to take into account the tension present on the entire West Coast during the hectic early days of 1942. Blackouts were mandatory and volunteer civilian lookouts scanned the skies nightly. There were at least two air raids by an aircraft launched from a Japanese submarine. There was submarine shore bombardment near Santa Barbara, and there were several submarine attacks on coastal shipping.

As dinner came to a close, there was the perennial speculation on a favorite topic. "What's next?"

Someone learned from the ship's aviators, temporarily stationed across the Bay at Alameda, that they probably would soon come aboard. This news was greeted by groans. The return of the scouting planes and their crews usually indicated a new operation.

We newcomers soon learned the reason. The sea time was tolerated. Evidently, it was the loss of shore leave that rankled. In port, the crew had one overnight leave every four days, and a leave up at midnight half way between. This last was the famously prized "Cinderella Liberty." Much fun and romance was to be found on the "beach," especially in San Francisco!

Most of our crew had just completed a twenty-seven-day cruise during the Battle of the Coral Sea, and they had their fill of the sea for awhile. This so-called

Christmas Island Cruise was a supporting operation of Task Force 1, commanded by Vice Admiral William S. Pye, a former temporary commander of the Pacific Fleet, and was the first since the war's beginning in which the battleships operated together. (They, of course, were no strangers to each other from operations during the peacetime years).

I had just completed twenty-three years at liberty. As a youth, I watched the ships steam over the horizon to destinations I could only imagine. I may have tried to appear blasé, but that latest news from the aviators was too stimulating for me to conceal. My excited comments quickly drew the teasing and jibes from Ensign McGowan to me. It hurt. I slowly learned in the months following to refrain from presenting myself as a target.

The next day was tour day for NROTC classmates Robert Sproul, Jr., Robert Yelland, and myself. They were assigned to communications, and I was sent to the Fifth Division in the gunnery department.

I was given an introductory tour of the secondary battery casemates by our division officer, Lieutenant (jg.) J. N. McNaughton, USNR. Although these spaces were new to me, I still felt somewhat at home for BB-46 was identical to BB-45.

Mr. McNaughton led me through the 5-inch magazines below the armored deck, and we inspected the complex series of hoists and conveyor belts which brought the shell and powder to the guns. After climbing the long ladders in the cage foremast, we looked over the two 5-inch gun fire control directors. This was secondary forward, and it was to be our battle station for many months.

We lowered the wind shields and admired the spectacular San Francisco scene. The foretops and some maintops of six old battleships towered above nearby pier warehouses. USS *Colorado* (BB-45), USS *New Mexico* (BB-40), USS *Mississippi* (BB-41), USS *Idaho* (BB-42), plus Pearl Harbor veterans USS *Pennsylvania* (BB-38), and USS *Tennessee* (BB-43), rose and fell with the tides. Their people, and *Maryland*'s people, worked and drilled during the days and made wonderful liberties through the nights. We seven were the only heavy gunnery ships available in the Pacific after the disaster at Pearl Harbor. The Japanese had eleven.

Survivors of the terrible Battle of Pearl Harbor . . . What could be more traumatic than the experience of a peacetime Sunday suddenly shattered by the rain of bombs and the explosions of torpedoes? Within me was growing a near-reverent feeling for my new ship and its company.

Lieutenant McNaughton was aboard *Maryland* on December 7, 1941. He told how Leslie Short, Seaman 1/c, with a 50-caliber machine gun, was one of the first in the entire fleet to take the attacking aircraft under fire. He described how *Oklahoma,* alongside to port, quickly capsized. From their lofty stations, *Maryland*'s gun fire control people watched USS *West Virginia* (BB-48), on the port quarter, and USS *California* (BB-44), ahead to starboard, slowly sink at their moorings, victims of torpedoes delivered early in the battle. His accounts of the gallant struggle made by USS *Nevada* (BB-36) to get to sea while under nearly constant attack, and of USS *Arizona*'s (BB-39) explosion and destruction, were graphic and memorable.

Maryland opened with her 5-inch 25-caliber anti-aircraft guns at the approaching high altitude bombers. He showed me then-unrepaired holes in the superstructure made by fragments flying from *Maryland*'s bomb hit on the fore-castle. *Maryland* had fired an amazing 7,450 rounds of antiaircraft ammunition with possibly five aircraft downed.

Leslie Short, S1c, 6B Division: "On the morning of December 7th I was in a machine gun tub which held three machine guns. It was in front of the conning tower, right over Turret II, on the signal bridge level. That gun tub was my work station as I was a seaman first class gun striker. It was my job, of course, to take care of the guns, keep the station clean, paint the deck, scrub and chip, and all that business.

"Well, to get a little privacy aboard ship sometimes is kinda hard. That gun tub was kinda ideal, because hardly anybody ever came around there, except somebody from the signal bridge, or, well, like the admiral used to walk around there quite a bit.

"On Sundays, when we got out to Pearl, I started sleeping up there at night on a cot under a little work bench. So, in the morning I'd pick up my cot, put it down in the magazine, go down and have breakfast, come back, and that morning I was writing some letters, addressing Christmas cards.

"The USS *Maryland* was facing west, and I was sitting at this table which faced east. The first Japanese planes came in from the southeast, kinda out of the sun. They were dive bombers, and they were diving on Ford Island. I remember seeing the smoke and debris and everything flying up in the air, but I cannot remember any sound.

"My 'take cover' station was down on the boat deck, which was down three ladders and back behind the signal bridge. I got half-way down the second ladder, and, for some reason, I turned around, went up to the signal bridge, and back to the gun tub. I uncovered a gun, got out a can of ammunition, and loaded up.

"By that time the dive bombers had stopped, and a torpedo plane came in across the bow of the *Oklahoma*. I opened fire on him. As it swept across the bow of our ship, it had caught fire and was smoking, so I swung back to the left again, toward the *Oklahoma*. Here came another one, and I opened fire on it. It started smoking, and I ran out of ammunition.

"There's two hundred rounds in a can. That's twenty seconds worth of fire power, because the 50-caliber machine gun fires six hundred rounds per minute."

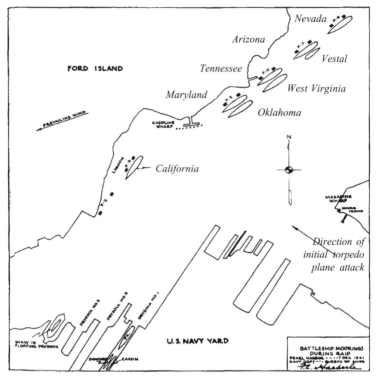

Pearl Harbor with positions of battleships on the morning of December 7, 1941.

Firman Balza, S1c, 5th Division: "Prior to the attack, I was standing on the gallery deck and was talking to a first class gunner's mate named Joe Klemcak and a first class cook named Rocky Halstead. We were wondering how it would be if we were attacked by the Japanese and if they sank a ship in the harbor, which could have blocked the channel and not allowed any of our ships to go to sea.

"We were standing there looking out over Ford Island. Just about that time, a Japanese Val dive bomber came down over the island and proceeded over the top of the buildings to the seaplane hanger, which was on one end of the island. As he turned and pulled up, he dropped his bomb. There was a very large red ball of fire and a black cloud of smoke. Then, all hell broke loose!

"It seemed as though the whole area was being hit all at one time.

"Immediately, I went into number three casemate, which was my battle station, and put the battle port into the porthole. I happened to be the trainer on number three broadside gun. I trained the gun out into the passageway on the gallery deck, but immediately realized that I was only blocking traffic. People running down the gallery deck were having to duck under the gun. I cranked it back into its secured position realizing that with the broadside battery we wouldn't be doing any shooting.

"I recall Rocky Halstead yelling: 'It's the damn Japs! With that, we just plain dispersed, and, of course, about that time they passed the word: 'All hands man your battle stations!'

"The guns were going, and just about then we had a hit on the forecastle. We lost our electricity because the hit knocked out the forward switchboard. It also knocked out the forward air compressor which supplied the guns so the ammunition had to be handled by hand.

"We formed a human chain from the third deck all the way up to the boat deck through the amidship casemate, and that's the way we got the ammunition up from the magazines.

"We were shooting back at the Japanese, and, by then, the *Oklahoma* had taken five direct torpedo hits. She was tied up to us on our port side, and she rolled over — capsized — right there in the harbor.

"Many of the fellows who got off the *Oklahoma* climbed up on cargo nets we had thrown over the side. They were covered with oil and, consequently, our ship became quite contaminated with all that oil. People were sliding around on that stuff.

West Virginia, *left, and* Tennessee *with rescue craft dodging blazing fuel in foreground.* West Virginia *was later raised* (Tennessee *suffered minor damage*), *and both ships, after repair and modernization, fought later in the war. Naval Historical Center.*

"The *California* was sunk and lost quite a few personnel.[2] The *West Virginia* burned very, very badly as she sank — probably one of the worst fires in the harbor. She seemed to be burning from the waterline clear to the foretop. The most tragic disasters were the *Arizona,* blown up completely, and the capsized *Oklahoma* with about six hundred people trapped inside. For days afterwards we had our rescue parties over there cutting holes so they could send people down into the compartments to rescue as many as possible."

The Pearl Harbor veterans' stories were overwhelming. Their anger was strong, as was their determination to make *Maryland* as ready as possible for revenge against the Japanese enemy. Those grand old ships were their pride — their seagoing homes.

---

[2] *Blue Water Beat: The Two Lives of the Battleship USS California* by George F. Gruner, published by The Glencannon Press, provides the complete history of that ship.

2

UNDERWAY!

"**N**ow, make all preparations for getting under-way at zero eight hundred." The voice was different but the words and inflection were the same as those stirring words which announced the beginning of our search for Amelia Earhart almost five years before.

The giant mooring lines, which were doubled, re-doubled, and equipped with rat guards, were singled up and the guards stowed. The boats were hoisted in and secured.

"Now, set the special sea detail." Many of the officers and men had specific duties assigned as part of the special sea detail, such as the forecastle ground tackle, in the chains with the sounding leads, in steering aft, on the signal bridge and in the pilot house. When ordered, others fell in at quarters.

The engineers had lighting-off and warm-up procedures well in advance so they could answer engine orders somewhat ahead of the underway time.

"The officer-of-the-deck is shifting his watch to the bridge."

"Testing the main engines."

"Testing the whistle and siren." Three ascending siren notes were followed by a steam whistle blast.

With the commanding officer, Captain D.C. Godwin, USN,[1] and the harbor pilot standing together on the bridge, the brow was hoisted out, the after lines taken in, and the stern worked away from the pier. At 0800 the last line came in, steaming colors were hoisted, and a long whistle blast sounded. The engines were put astern, and we slowly backed away. The ship's band struck up a lively march.

Wow! Would the old salts forgive my huge grin?

The deck vibrated under our feet, and the stack gases poured out with increasing velocity as the throttles were eased open. No black smoke, mind you, especially from us. We were the flagship of the task group's commander, Rear Admiral W.S. Anderson, USN.

As we backed into the stream with the bow steadying on a heading toward the Golden Gate, *Colorado* fell in astern. We joined the three-destroyer screen and sortied on the mission assigned by Vice Admiral William S. Pye, USN.

Acting on a report that a small Japanese aircraft carrier might be approaching the coast, we steamed to a

---

[1] Captain Godwin was the commander of our Naval Reserve Officers Training Corps unit at the University of California in Berkeley just prior to the war. He was lost in an air crash while returning to the United States after his tour in *Maryland*. Commander Chester W. Nimitz, USN, founded this NROTC unit in 1926 and was its first commanding officer.

point 650 nautical miles, bearing 300 degrees true, from San Francisco. The chart showed we were now on a logical enemy approach track for an aircraft raid on our home port.

We found only empty seas. Instead of an end-around slash at the West Coast, the Japanese commander, Admiral Yamamoto, dispatched his diversion force to attack and invade targets in the Aleutians. It consisted of two carriers, *Ryujo* and *Junyo*, plus transports and screen.

We patrolled the area until joined on June 6th by Admiral Pye and the remaining ships of Task Force 1. The re-formed Task Force 1 then consisted of seven battleships, eight destroyers, and a recent addition to the Pacific Fleet, USS *Long Island* (CVE-1), the Navy's first escort carrier.

With air cover provided by *Long Island*'s twelve F4F-4 Wildcat fighters, plus her search aircraft and our OS2Us, we steamed west in support of our forces at Midway and in the Aleutian Islands.

(text continues on p. 21)

THE OS2U

The quarterdeck, captain's sanctuary in port, erupts with intense activity whenever "Flight Quarters" sounds. The deck crews lower the lifelines, man the cranes and the rescue motor whaleboat. The plane crew removes the covers, frees the controls, and checks the plane to be launched. It is quickly manned by the pilot and radioman.

The catapult launching officer supervises the loading of the 5-inch powder cartridge. One catapult is on the quarterdeck with the other mounted atop Turret III. Two aircraft are carried on the catapults, the third is usually stored on a wheeled cradle, secured to the deck. The launching officer then checks the placement of the retaining ring at the rear of the launching car, in the cradle of which rests the aircraft's center pontoon, and satisfies himself the catapult car's safety stops are in place for the engine's start and warm-up.

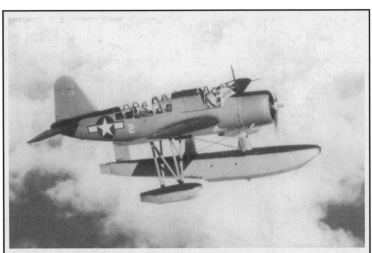

Maryland's OS2U spotting and observation aircraft.   Author.

Meanwhile the OTC (Officer in Tactical Command) brings the task group to a course which puts the apparent wind[2] broad on the port or starboard bow.   When the pilot signals ready, the catapult officer orders the catapult trained into the wind.   This done, he takes a position on deck in the pilot's sight and in that of the kneeling catapult gunner who holds the firing lanyard at just the correct tension.   With the bridge's permission, the catapult officer orders the car's safety stops withdrawn.   He signals the pilot to "rev up."   As the engine revolutions mount, the pilot places his head firmly against his headrest.   The radioman has two grips.   He grasps those and bends his head down.   They wait.

The catapult launching officer is a lonely figure as he stands there, his right arm extended and parallel to the deck.   His job, like many shipboard jobs, may not appear difficult, but it must be done right every time.

The engine snarls and the only restraint is that small metal ring, perhaps an inch and one-half in diameter.   The catapult officer has his eye on a portion of the ship against the horizon.   The ship rolls down.   A pause.   Slowly, slowly, the ship starts up.   His arm sweeps down.   The lanyard is yanked,
WHAM!

[2] Apparent wind is the wind direction created by the combination of the actual wind and that caused by the movement of the vessel through the water.

The small ring parts. The aircraft leaps ahead. The car stops abruptly against hydraulic buffers. As the plane continues, perhaps it may dip slightly, then, it's up and away!

The aircraft recovery process starts with the streaming of a sled, usually to port. Affixed to its trailing edge is a rope net, perhaps six feet long and as wide as the sled.

While the plane circles, the ship's conning officer brings the wind on the port bow. He then swings the ship's head through the wind and steadies her course with the wind on the starboard bow. Skilled ship handling creates a slick heading directly upwind. The slick formed as the hull slides through the turn is surprisingly smooth, even in fairly rough weather.

The plane quickly alights in the quiet stretch. Safely down, the pilot opens the throttle, and, steering with the plane's rudder, plus a small pontoon rudder, he aims for the sled's center. There, he cuts the throttle. The aircraft drops back until a hook, which automatically extends from the pontoon's keel, catches the rope net.

The waiting crane operator lowers his weighted hook to the standing radioman. With the aircraft's hoisting sling engaged, the engine is killed, and the craneman deftly hoists her in.

Usually, aircraft operations went about as described. Interesting, if never seen before, but quickly routine, unless one of several possible difficulties occurred.

An outlaw wave, for example, could give the ship an unusual roll just at the launching moment. A hangfire might delay the cartridge explosion. If shot too late on the uproll, the pilot may find himself struggling to prevent a stall. It must have been horrendous to go on the down roll straight into the face of an oncoming sea.

Or, picture the following: Seeing the catapult officer's signal, the pilot, head against his headrest, revs his engine. The catapult officer's arm is outstretched, ready to drop. The ship is almost at the bottom of its downward roll . . .

Suddenly, the pilot notes a change in his engine feel or sound — perhaps a broken valve stem. He instinctively turns toward the officer on deck to halt the launch.

Too late! That arm is sweeping down. They are on their way, with the pilot receiving a blow from the accelerating headrest against the side of his head.

If the weather deteriorates while operating close to land, the aircraft merely flies to a shore base. It is a different matter

Third generation photos are all that's available of Maryland's OS2U coming back on board. Left, approaching hook, below, being lifted aboard. Author.

when the ship is far at sea. When the seas are high, the skilled aviator alights as close to the ship as possible. This shortens the taxi, and he stays in the temporarily smooth water. If he lands too far away, or delays for any reason, he is guaranteed a contest against the oncoming seas as the slick disappears.

The engine roars, and the spray flies as the pilot guns her over each crest. He then must quickly cut back as they plunge into the troughs, or they'll dig on in. Each throttle-cut loses them distance, so he fiercely blasts through the next swell's top. It's a wild battle. Our conning officer helps by slowing the ship, but he must maintain steerageway.

One problem is the correct choice of a recovery course after the plane has landed and is taxiing up to the sled. If the wind is directly on the bow, the seas will cause the aircraft to rise and fall many feet after the slick has gone. This complicates the engagement of the pontoon hook to the rope net, and it renders the craneman's and the radioman's work onerous — nearly impossible. If they do manage to hook on, the plane will come out of the water with a jerk that threatens serious structural damage, the parting of the lifting line, or worse.

Now, if a course is chosen which brings the wind too far around on the starboard beam, there will be a good lee, but the roll of the ship will be too great. The boom rises and falls. There is again the possibility for a tremendous jerk.

Adjustment of the ship's recovery course while the aircraft taxis up presents a difficulty as the plane may sheer too far out, or, worse, into the ship's side, if not carefully fended off. The good seaman at the conn selects the best possible course the first time.

If all goes well, the pontoon finally bangs down on the sled. The throttle is backed off. If that hook catches, fine. If it misses, the aircraft falls aft, and the struggle resumes . . .

We never begrudged battleship and cruiser aviators their flight pay, and some suggested they also be given pay for submarine duty.

(continued from p. 17)

Battle line maneuvers require meticulous planning. The cruising formation selected by the admiral and his staff is important. Depending on the conditions, it may be changed, but air and submarine defense must always be considered. In the situation that existed on June 6, 1942, ease of deployment into a line of battle was a basic factor.

Our cruising formation, therefore, was three columns abreast. On the left flank, *Maryland*, as flagship of Battleship Division 4, steamed along, with *Colorado* in column astern. Probably 2,000 yards on our starboard beam rode *Pennsylvania*, Admiral Pye's Task Force 1 flagship. Astern was *Tennessee*. Battleship Division 3 flagship, *New Mexico,* with *Mississippi* and *Idaho* in column astern, was stationed about 2,000 yards on *Pennsylvania*'s starboard beam. The destroyers, except one, were usually in a bent line screen ahead, and *Long Island* maneuvered astern in her flight operations. Astern of her and slightly to starboard was her destroyer plane guard.

For drill, as we cruised west, Admiral Pye decided to form his ships in a line of battle — a column, or line

Colorado, Maryland *and* West Virginia *lead the battle line during fleet exercises in the late 1920s. Naval Historical Center.*

ahead, usually — and do it by divisions. Colorful signal pennants and flags climbed partway to *Pennsylvania*'s yardarms; they flew at the dip. *Colorado* hoisted hers, momentarily at the dip, then all the way up. She was at the end of the chain of signal responsibility and this indicated she understood and would comply. Following her action, we quickly two-blocked our hoists. The same actions took place in Battleship Division 3, and also in *Tennessee*. Then the escort commander signaled directions to the other destroyers for their new screening stations or column assignments.

By then, all the officers-of-the-deck and their assistants had consulted the signal book and interpreted the directions sent; they informed the captains and alerted engineering main control for coming speed changes. The main control watches warned the firerooms, and, if this were an actual battle situation, they would have ordered all boilers lighted off and put on the line.

With all the hoists two-blocked, *Pennsylvania*'s hoists moved up to the yardarms. The word then came from the admiral or his representative:

"Execute!" All the signal hoists quickly disappeared.

Maryland and *Colorado* maintained their course and probably their speed. *Pennsylvania* and *New Mexico* both turned left to courses their conning officers determined from their maneuvering boards, or from "seaman's eye." *Tennessee* and *Mississippi* turned left and followed when they reached *Pennsylvania*'s and *New Mexico*'s wakes. *Idaho* turned left and followed when she reached *New Mexico*'s and *Mississippi*'s wake.

Speed adjustments usually have to be made to attain the assigned interval between ships, and this is the tricky part. Battleship Division 4 steams right along, but the other conning officers are working with thousands and thousands of tons, and momentum is an extremely important factor. If, for example, extra turns are put on to close the distance, they must be taken off in time so as not to over-correct. And vice versa.

Only experience will dictate to the conning officers when to put the rudders over for that last turn into column. Speed is also a consideration here, as the rudders require varying times to act at different speeds.

We soon had a fine column of ships, and it is fairly simple — well, maybe not "simple" but it can be done — if everyone knows how. Imagine how it was in the first World War's Battle of Jutland, on May 31, 1916, when British Admiral Jellicoe took, not seven, but *twenty-four* battleships into column. This, while he commenced firing on German Admiral Scheer's High Seas Fleet!

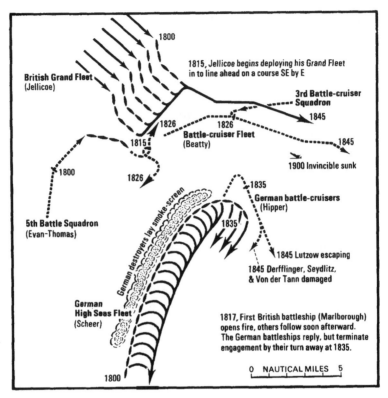

1800

1815, Jellicoe begins deploying his Grand Fleet
in to line ahead on a course SE by E

British Grand Fleet
(Jellicoe)

3rd Battle-cruiser
Squadron

1845

1826   1826

1826

Battle-cruiser Fleet
(Beatty)

1845

1815

1900 Invincible sunk

1800   1826

1835

German battle-cruisers
(Hipper)

1835

5th Battle Squadron
(Evan-Thomas)

German destroyers lay smoke-screen

1845 Lutzow escaping

1845 Derfflinger, Seydlitz,
& Von der Tann damaged

German
High Seas Fleet
(Scheer)

1817, First British battleship (Marlborough)
opens fire, others follow soon afterward.
The German battleships reply, but terminate
engagement by their turn away at 1835.

0   NAUTICAL MILES   5

1800

In the Battle of Jutland (May 31, 1916) during World War I, Admiral Jellicoe formed a battle line and executed the classic maneuver of "Crossing the T" on the approaching German Fleet under Admiral Scheer. Battleships and Battlecruisers.

By June 10th we reached a position about 1,650 miles equidistant from the battle areas at Midway and Kiska. Task Force 1 did not participate in either action, but it fulfilled that time-honored function of "fleet in being." The possible presence of such a fleet must be included in the calculations of the enemy commander.

Returning to San Francisco, *Maryland* berthed at Pier 7 and the crew again enjoyed the evenings ashore. At another pier was the new battleship, USS *North Carolina* (BB-55), just in from the East Coast. Her long, graceful

USS North Carolina *at sea, June 3, 1945. National Archives.*

bow, her nine 16-inch guns in three turrets, her many twin-mount 5-inch 38-caliber dual purpose guns together with her vast supply of 40mm and 20mm automatic weapons, aroused mixed feelings of pride and envy in the old battle-ship crews.

We didn't see much more of her because she and the other new battleships, when they arrived in the Pacific, operated with the fast carrier task forces. This was something the prewar battleships such as *Maryland* couldn't do. When combat-loaded and in warm waters, the older ships found it difficult to maintain an eighteen-knot fleet speed. The warmer ocean water running through the turbines' steam condensers made them less efficient, reducing the power output.

Several weeks later, we sailed for another west-ward cruise during which *Maryland* was ordered into Pearl Harbor. The ship's company was silent as we entered and moored. It was only seven months since that history-altering event and all eyes were on the exposed bottom of capsized *Oklahoma* and the sad remains of *Arizona*.

When Rear Admiral Harry W. Hill, USN, took command of Battleship Division 4, he had two ships whose material condition was ready for combat. Captain Godwin was still our commanding officer as *Maryland* made final preparations for the move to a more advanced base.

Main and secondary batteries aboard *Maryland* and *Colorado* could obtain target information from either the foretop or the maintop. To compensate for the weight of the 40mm Bofors and 20mm Oerlikon antiaircraft guns added at Pearl Harbor and to give a broader field of fire, the maintops were removed. The aircraft catapults atop Turret III and the two boat deck secondary battery guns from each ship were also landed. The 20mm mounts emplaced on the turrets and in tubs atop the shortened mainmasts had impressive fields of fire from the horizon past the zenith, and all the way around from forward of the starboard beam, over the stern, to forward of the port beam.

Each ship's main battery now had two gun fire control positions topside: Spot I in the foretop and Spot III in the conning tower. Our secondary batteries were left with the directors in secondary forward. One controlled the remaining four starboard guns, the other the four to port. I was the port gun control officer.

Whenever we entered or left port, the guns were manned against possible submarine attack. Secondary battery guns still had telescopic pointer and trainer sights. During our sortie, I heard laughing and joking over the gun control telephones. Our departure through the channel passed a housing development. Glancing over the side, we noted the guns were trained out together, but slightly converged. As we watched, they slowly swung aft as we stood down the channel. Following the gun line of sight with my 7 x 50 glass, there stood a lovely young lady in a white dress — arms and legs tanned, a flower in her hair.

She had stepped from her kitchen door to wave good-bye.

The thought came later that dozens of ships were moving through that channel. Sailors being sailors, she had hundreds of telescopic sighted guns pointed her way. A veritable Mary Martin of that sea-channel, she probably lived on in the many gunners' memories who carried her bright image to all the desolate or beautiful corners of the Pacific.

She was the last girl we saw for many months. For those lost in the sunken ships, and for those killed in the returned ships, she was the last girl they ever saw.

3

In the Doldrums: Fiji and New Hebrides

W e were aware, as we departed Pearl Harbor in November 1942, that almost everything was in short supply. But we were well provided with clear indications (new antiaircraft weapons, stores, fuel, and, especially, a destroyer escort) that the high command expected that our 16-inch guns would be needed in the desperate sea fighting off Guadalcanal. There, our losses were heavy in the lightly armored cruisers and destroyers. The new battleship USS *South Dakota* (BB-49) sustained forty-two gunfire hits, some heavy caliber, and *North Carolina* was torpedoed by a submarine.

We did not know of the damages at the time but were convinced we were headed for battle by the words of

Captain Godwin as we crossed the Equator: we were to perfect our combat skills and we should be prepared for possible casualties.

An additional indication of our destination was provided by a war correspondent's morning visit to our foretop station. He was Richard Tregaskis, author of the soon-to-be-famous book, *Guadalcanal Diary*. Having spent many days with the Marines on Guadalcanal, he told us much about the conditions there: the heat, humidity, rain, mud, insects, fevers; shortages of food, clothing, even ammunition. He praised the dogged fighting abilities of the United States Marines, and described the determination of the Japanese soldiers, and the severe effect on our troops' morale when they underwent bombardment by Japanese naval vessels.

Admiral Yamamoto had lost battleships *Kirishima* and *Hiei* but he had many more heavy ships immediately available. Nevertheless, he chose not to commit them, and, because *North Carolina*, after quick repair at Pearl Harbor, was able to rejoin the fast-moving and hard-hitting new USS *Washington* (BB-56) in close support of the Solomons operations, we were diverted to a standby anchorage in Nandi Waters, Fiji Islands. Our heavy gun

USS Indiana *(BB-53) as she appeared in September, 1942. U.S. Naval Photographic Center.*

power was further strengthened by the January arrival of the new battleship USS *Indiana* (BB-53).

Battleship Division 4 was based in the Fiji Islands from late November 1942, until February 1943. *Maryland* and *Colorado* were then ordered to Efate Island in the New Hebrides. After more than six months there we moved up to Espiritu Santo, also in the New Hebrides.

It was a trying time in the war's backwaters. All those months waiting for something to happen seemed to last forever.

During its early 1941 expansion, the Navy had severe shortages in people, aircraft, equipment, and parts. Admiral Ernest J. King, USN, was commander-in-chief of the Atlantic Fleet. Undaunted, he issued orders, "Make the best of what you have."

Lieutenant McNaughton, who remained our secondary battery officer for much of World War II, followed the spirit of this policy in an exemplary manner. Never once did we hear him complain about our guns, ammunition, and gun fire control equipment. He corrected what he could and encouraged us to do our best with the rest.

We also had a special problem: the 5-inch 51-caliber gun was designed for defense against destroyer and submarine attacks. But this was a new type of warfare. We could not elevate sufficiently to engage the horizontal, glide, or dive bomber. Also, the fifty-pound shell was loaded and rammed by hand, as was the cloth bag containing the propelling powder. Even if we could elevate the guns for antiaircraft fire, we couldn't load at the higher angles.

Lt. McNaughton found a way to adapt our guns to anti-torpedo plane fire. We could elevate enough to engage an incoming torpedo plane, but we had no time-of-flight computer. We also lacked the fuse-setting mechanism required to detonate the shell as it intercepts the target.

"Mr. Mac" procured ten rounds per gun of 5-inch 38-caliber antiaircraft shells and directed the fuses be set at two seconds for a barrage. (Later, the radio proximity fuse solved this time-of-flight problem. It contained a tiny radio transmitter which began to transmit as soon as the shell was fired. If the signal was reflected by a target, the fuse's radio receiver instantly detonated the shell with excellent results.)

Mr. Mac also computed the gunsight lead settings and had them painted on each gun. Antiaircraft fire, of course, presents the same problem faced by a hunter attempting to down a bird on the wing. To allow for the missile's time in flight, the gun must be fired the correct angle ahead of an aircraft crossing the line of sight.

Given the setup, the procedure was fairly simple. Each gun captain selected the incoming target and coached the pointer and trainer on. He also estimated the target angle (the relative bearing of the firing ship as seen from the target) and gave this figure to the gun sightsetter, who, after consulting the table painted on the gun, set up the proper lead.

As soon as the pointer settled on the target, he closed his firing key, locked it, and followed the plane in. When the gun captain estimated the range to be about twenty-five hundred yards, he signalled the plugman to load. As soon as the breech plug closed, off the round would go.

The instant the gun returned to battery the plugman would have the plug wide open. (Most of them "rode the plug."[1]) He inserted a new primer and the trayman emplaced his tray to protect the precisely machined interrupted-screw threads. The spongeman then reached in and swabbed off the mushroom — the breech plug part which

---

[1] The plugman can open the breech plug faster by holding the operating handle during the gun's recoil.

Gun crew of No. 4 5-inch 51-caliber Broadside Gun: (l. to r.) Holderlein, Gun Captain; Keesee, Plugman; Ellis, Sightsetter; Click, 1st Shellman; Mollner, 2nd Shellman; McIllroy, 1st Powderman; Sims, Trayman; Judy, Spongeman; Johns, Rammerman; Dendy, Pointer and Gamblin, Trainer.   During combat everyone wore helmets and lifejackets.   Note sight settings for anti-torpedo plane fire painted on the gun just over the captain's left shoulder.   Author.

abutted against the sensitive black powder end of the propellant bag. A burning ember from the previous charge would be particularly dangerous there, as the gas ejection air used to scour the powder chamber after each round doesn't act on the open mushroom face.

Then the shellman — usually the gun crew's largest and strongest — slammed in the next shell, seating its copper rotating band as solidly as possible in the rifling's inboard end.

The rammerman anxiously searched the powder chamber for burning embers not ejected by the forced air system. If he missed a tiny spark, it could flame the powder bag and incinerate the entire crew. That's called

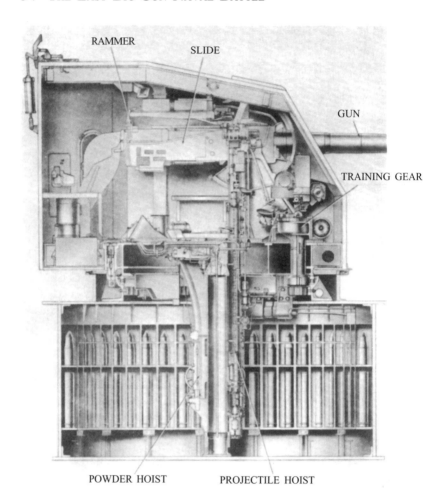

RAMMER SLIDE GUN TRAINING GEAR POWDER HOIST PROJECTILE HOIST

Longitudinal section of a typical 5-inch/38 gun mount showing general arrangement and details of the mount. U.S. Navy.

a "flareback." Then he rammed the shell home with his combination sponge and rammer. That done, he took one last look and called:

"Bore clear!"

The first powderman then took the naked powder bag from where he was shielding it against sparks with his body and slid it into the powder chamber.

Tray out; breech closed.

"Wham!" Round two on the way!

It is that mighty instant, when the charge ignites, and the projectile speeds on its way, which welds most gunners into a lasting brotherhood.

The heavy breech came walloping back as if it meant to shoulder its way past the crew and smash through the inboard bulkhead. It was a moment no one was likely to forget: the flash, the blasts, the smoke. . . That breech halted without fail, however, due to the massive recoil cylinders, and slid quickly and smoothly back to battery.

We drilled, drilled, drilled. Mr. Mac and Lt. (j.g.) Frank Springer, our new Fifth Division Officer, were determined we would be the best gunners anywhere. As junior division officer, I was on the boat deck beside the loading machine every working day. There were grumbles. We drilled past the point athletes know as "staleness." We drilled at every possible casualty. We drilled with men in other men's positions. We drilled on to a condition where every man was forever at ease in his function.

Later, in combat areas, we were always ready for anti-torpedo plane fire, but the enemy aircraft would be too high; their range too great; the range fouled by screening destroyers; planes identified as friendly just in time. There were dozens of air-defense general quarters, but no targets for us.

Our chance finally came, a plane coming in low on the port bow, a real Japanese sucker, first jinking, then flying straight and steady, as they must. There was his torpedo, slung below the fuselage, ready to drop. On he came and we saw our gun barrels following him. The range was clear; we told the four gun captains to go ahead. And did they shoot!

Wham! Wham! Wham! Whamity-wham! Those thirty-year-old guns, built for another war and other targets,

Nakajima B5N Kate (replica), Japanese torpedo plane. American History Illustrated.

let go almost in unison, fifty-six men working with cool coordination.

Up and over that torpedo plane went, trailing smoke and flame into the sea!

The gunners leaped from their casemates, cheering and yelling wildly. They patted the hot muzzles of our long, beautiful guns, caressed the breeches.

In the tops we searched for more targets, but there was just that one. . .

Youngsters we were, with the old bag guns (so-called because the propelling charge came in bags) in old, slow *Maryland.* But now we felt like cavalrymen who had just overrun a machine gun. Jeered by the "real" antiaircraft gunners, we took our broadsiders into the age of air warfare.

Mr. McNaughton, pondering shore bombardments, foresaw that smoke and dust would quickly obscure the impact area. We would have to use the "offset" method in which the director is aimed at a known point in the clear. The guns are then offset in range and bearing to bring the shells onto the target.

The difficulty is that these offsets constantly vary as the firing vessel moves. We had no equipment to determine the changing values until Mr. Mac developed our own "iswas."[2]

Lieutenant McNaughton carried on by spiriting into the foretop two improved Mark 7 rangekeepers to replace our primitive Mark 2 "Baby Fords." Only old timers would appreciate that coup. Admirals King (Chief of Naval Operations) and Pye certainly would, as those two friends had worked together in 1908 on the development of an improved gunnery range (keeping) machine.

The bulky telephone helmets were a problem in the foretop's close quarters. Our ingenious leader soon modified the standard helmets so we could wear our telephone headsets under them.

It is imperative to mention Admiral Hill, who continued in command of Battleship Division 4 during that preparatory period. We quickly discovered his credo: "Make every effort to conduct training as much like combat as possible; we must accept the inherent risks." In the past we had done our firing practice by batteries — main, then secondary, then antiaircraft. Not so under Admiral Hill. "We may be engaged with all batteries, and probably with incoming fire."

So, when we came on the practice range during the darkest part of the night, the 5-inch 25-caliber AA would open with starshell behind the target for identification purposes, and the main battery would commence its one-minute salvos. Between each main battery blast, our secondary would fire four times rapidly. It was spectacular, and we did learn several important truths.

Most pertinent was the subsequent report from our main battery spotting officer in the foretop just above us,

---

[2] The ship *is* here now, it *was* there then. Calculating the difference corrected the difficulty.

Lieutenant James Dare, USN, USNA (United States Naval Academy), Class of 1939. He had, with Lieutenant Warren Lowerre, USN, USNA, Class of 1940, main battery plotting room officer, responsibility for early hits.

"The jar from the 5-inch salvos fouls my fire control radar scope so I can't get a return signal from the main battery shell splashes. Without this signal I can't spot onto the target."

If we were to obtain maximum effectiveness, this difficulty would have to be considered. Depending on the situation, it might be well to hold secondary battery fire during an action's early stages.

(Combat reports later indicated that everyone fired everything as fast as they could in the limited time usually available.)

Inspired by Admiral Hill's emphasis on training realism, we discussed another gunnery situation unique to combat: A stipulated number of rounds are usually ordered for a peacetime target shoot. The practice ends with the guns unloaded, unless there had been a misfire. This wasn't the case in action. Guns fire until the target is destroyed, until it leaves the battery's firing arc, or it moves out of range. The gun crews automatically reload after each round.

In combat, if a control officer orders "cease fire" without warning he will probably have one or more loaded guns. He has a problem. Loaded hot guns sometimes "cook off."[3] If a naval force is attempting to disappear after a night engagement, nothing could be more disconcerting than to have one of its guns suddenly fire; the blast is visible for miles. Also, a friendly ship could be endangered by that stray round. (A ship in the Battle of Surigao Strait experienced this problem.)

---

[3] The heat from the hot metal can detonate either the explosive in the primer or the sensitive black powder ignition charge in the base of the powder bag.

To prevent such an incident, we developed the following procedure: Upon receipt of a cease-fire order, we ordered the gun captains: "Check fire, check fire; all guns acknowledge."

Came the quick response:

"Gun 2, aye; Gun 4, aye; Gun 6, aye; Gun 8, aye."

"Now stand by to unload through the muzzles. Do NOT reload. Do NOT reload, all guns acknowledge."

"Gun 2, aye; Gun 4, aye. . . .

During the pause, the director pointer and trainer remained on the target, or, if there were no longer a target, they kept clear of friendly ships as we maneuvered. The gun pointers and trainers kept their pointers matched, and the guns swung with the director.

Upon seeing a nod from the secondary battery officer after he received the usual permission from the bridge, I sent down again: "Stand by to unload through the muzzles. Do NOT reload. I repeat: Do NOT reload. All guns acknowledge."

"Gun 2, aye; Gun 4, aye. . . ."

"Resume fire, resume fire!"

When I pointed my finger at the director buzzerman, he closed his key. The buzzers sounded in the top and in all the casemates. The director pointer then closed his firing key.

Wham!

"Cease fire, cease fire! All guns report empty."

"Gun 2, empty; Gun 4, empty . . ."

We tried using the phrase, "All guns report unloaded," but that led to transmission errors. "Empty" was easily understood.

We repeated this procedure hundreds of times. Tiresome and boring it was, but it paid off in the same execution of the coming torpedo plane, bombardment and counterbattery actions.

As the months passed, more ships became available and Admiral Hill was able to form Task Force 11. On patrol this force consisted of three new escort carriers, *Suwanee, Chenango* and *Sangamon,* with *Maryland, Colorado,* and screening destroyers.

Unsung we were, because Task Force 11 never saw action. Admiral Hill, however, drilled us into an efficient unit which would, we felt, be of good use against the enemy. Although we weren't the fastest task force around, we now had about everything else: fighter cover, torpedo planes, strong antiaircraft defenses, good radar, sixteen 16-inch guns, and our two battleships had excellent torpedo protection. Since they were converted tankers, our three carriers were probably more durable than many of their sisters.

We operated in a tightly closed circle so we could give the carriers antiaircraft support, and they could give the task force good fighter coverage. In addition to routine zigzags, we practiced simultaneous emergency turns to the right and to the left in defense against simulated submarine and aircraft attack. Deck loads of fighters were launched

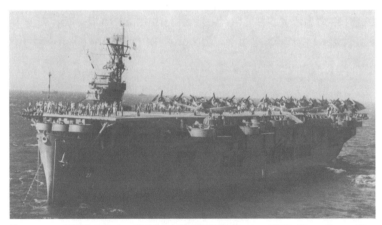

Suwanee *(CVE-27) in 1944 with F6F* Hellcats, *SBD* Dauntless *dive bombers and TBM* Avenger *torpedo bombers on her flight deck.* National Archives.

against incoming unidentified targets — some simulated, and against other radar targets which may have been the real thing.

At such close range, it was splendid to see the fighters leaping into the air as we all swung into the wind. One by one those small planes went, tucking in their wheels as they headed for the high sky. The new fighter director officers, charged with the interception of enemy air raids, had unique opportunity to work with operational fighter pilots at sea. You may easily imagine the warm and friendly feeling we always had for those special flyers, as they orbited way above us, alone in their cockpits, poised and ready to pounce on any incoming "bandits."

Boredom, as always, was a factor to be considered. We manned those gun control circuits at general quarters every morning and evening at sea and during many battle drills in port. But, lightened by almost continuous banter and old-timer sea stories, we carried through.

We soon lost the escort carriers to other duties, but we became much better prepared for combat operations.

Our view from the foretop was splendid. There was almost always something going on in an underway task force: carrier landings and takeoffs; destroyers going alongside ship after ship delivering mail and passengers, fueling and provisioning.

The starboard battery gun control officer, Ensign "Dead-Eye" Jones, USNR, and I made a practice of describing these events to the people in the casemates below. Mr. Jones, the Fifth Division junior officer after I took over the division from Lieutenant Springer, was especially popular. A skilled jazz trumpet man, he often would take his trumpet up to the casemates after work and treat the division to concerts.

"Dead-Eye" earned his nickname among our small group of foretopmen for the *Maryland*'s most spectacular 5-inch shot. During one operation, when ceasing fire from a routine bombardment mission, one of his gun captains was off the phone. Some minor casualty. The gun captain came back on to report his gun was loaded and hot.

A search of the shoreline through his glass revealed a previously undamaged fuel storage tank. Mr. Jones put his director on the tank and made a quick range estimate. That last shell winged up, over, and directly through the roof of the target. The resultant explosion and tall plume of black smoke were most satisfying. The fire and smoke persisted for several days and the notable marksmanship of trumpeter Jones and his sharpshooting crew became part of the *Maryland*'s lore.

Since we were not equipped with optical or radar rangefinders in secondary forward, we often engaged in friendly range estimate competition. We made our estimates and called down to the fine stereo rangefinder in sky control for an accurate reading. One aid was to ob-

TBM-3, the torpedo plane which made simulated attacks on our ships. This is the aircraft later used by our naval aviators to assist in the sinking of Japanese battleships Yamato *and* Masashi. *Author.*

serve carefully a screening destroyer's position relative to the horizon. We had charts calculated for our height of eye. If a destroyer sat exactly on the horizon, it had to be at a known range. If the destroyer was steaming on our side of the horizon, and that horizon cut her bow half way up, we knew from our chart the range was a certain amount less, and so forth. This was, of course, useful only in daylight, but that and other drills sharpened our abilities, as demonstrated by Mr. Jones' remarkable one gun salvo — accurate within twenty feet at a range of several miles.

Never one to rest when there was a opportunity to improve his people's fighting efficiency, Admiral Hill somehow arranged for the busy fleet carriers to simulate aircraft dive bomb and torpedo attacks on our formation. This had been a peacetime exercise, but not during our war cruises.

Radar reported aircraft approaching — high.

We searched all the sky. Sometimes we would spot them; usually we couldn't as they skillfully used the sun's glare to blind us or hid among the towering cloud banks. Often, the first we saw was the flash of a wing as they rolled into a dive. They dived with perfect timing, mainly from out of the sun, but spreading in all directions.

Down they would come, twisting and turning.

No matter where you stood on deck or in the tops, they appeared to be aiming at you, and at you alone.

After eighteen — or thirty, or forty — dive bombers plummeted down, then heaved out with vapor streaming from their wingtips and their engines snarling, they'd be gone in the blink of an eye.

The last act was the torpedo plane phase. Unnoticed on the horizon, they maneuvered for the best attack positions. Then a dash toward us, simulated torpedo drops at close range from all directions, and skillful pull-ups that left us breathless. *(text continues on p. 46)*

SHIP NAMES

"What's in a name?" the poet asked. Much, I believe.

Victory, Warspite, Royal Oak, Indomitable, Indefatigable: these are names which inspire the English Navy. Many American ship names commemorate great events, great men, and great ships: *Constitution, Lexington, Nimitz* . . . And *Enterprise,* that incredible fleet carrier of World War II, which proudly carried the tradition of *Enterprise*, a sloop of war from the Revolutionary War.

American battleships were named after states of the Union — *California, Iowa, West Virginia. Maryland!* We liked our name — a sweet lady, a fine state and a happy ship.

Ours was the third to carry that name. First was a 380-ton sloop mounting thirty 9-pounders and six 6-pounders. She was built at the Price Shipyard in Baltimore, Maryland, launched June 3, 1799, and commissioned in August 1799, with Captain John Rodgers as commanding officer.

The French were searching and seizing merchant vessels trading in the British West Indies. American shipping interests applied to the United States government for protection. *Maryland* was immediately ordered south to an area called the Surinam station.

She cruised from French Guiana to Curaçao protecting U.S. shipping from attack by French privateers and warships. While so engaged she captured the schooner, *Clarissa,* an American slave trader without papers, and she recaptured the Portuguese brig, *Gloria da Mar,* taken by the French a few days before

Maryland was the only American warship in that area until August 1800, when she sailed for home. Repaired at Baltimore, her next important mission was the transport of Congressman John Dawson, President Adams' special representative to France. He carried the Pinckney Treaty designed to end the undeclared hostilities between France and the United States.

USS Maryland *(ACR-8) in Dewey drydock at Manila, circa 1908.
Mr. D.M. McPherson.*

The second was USS *Maryland* (ACR-8), a 13,680-
ton, 504-foot armored cruiser mounting two 18-inch torpedo
tubes and forty guns: four 8-inch, fourteen 6-inch, eighteen 3-
inch, and four 3-pounders. She was constructed by Newport
News Shipbuilding and Drydock Company, Virginia, and commissioned April 18, 1905, with Captain R.R. Ingersoll, USN,
commanding.

Notable voyages were survey missions to Alaska in
1912 and 1913 and a 1912 trip to Tokyo carrying Secretary of
State Knox to Emperor Meiji Tenno's funeral. *Maryland* also
supported American interests in Mexico and Nicaragua during
1913, 1914, and in 1916.

The Navy was planning a gigantic new 16-inch gunned
battle line, battleships to be named after states. The keel of the
first of these was to be laid in April, 1917, and it was desired
to name her *Maryland*.

Cruisers would be named for cities, so the armored
cruiser, *Maryland,* became *Frederick*, after a city in Maryland.

(continued from p. 43)

Maryland was leading *Colorado* into Efate after our interminable Fijis sojourn when a Marine Corsair fighter squadron was called in to make simulated strafing runs.

Great aircraft, new in those days, somewhat difficult to operate aboard the carriers, Corsairs were useful through World War II and into the Korean War. Gull-winged craft, they were sleek, fast and beautiful in a warlike way.

A genius named them. To see the Corsairs slicing through the air was to be reminded of the originals, the slim pirate vessels sliding to sea from the shelter of an island or coastal bluff to intercept a lumbering merchantman.

Here they come!

Suddenly, eighteen fast aircraft are making runs. Painted dark blue and knifing in from all sides, it is again

A Corsair on the deck of an aircraft carrier awaiting her turn to launch. Author.

the olden days with *Maryland* and *Colorado* the slow, fat, rich prizes.

As they zoomed in low on the water, and then up and away, we looked down into the cockpits. Then, tragedy. One Corsair completed a run and pulled up for another go-around, as a second came in low and fast.

They collided head-on before our shocked eyes. There was a huge, violent red burst with a black rim. As the black cloud drifted away, we in the foretop felt the loss, as if they were our own brothers. There they were in their beautiful machines, wild and free, full of glorious life. Now they were gone — poof — just like that.

The remaining planes formed up and disappeared over the horizon with two vacancies in the formation. Our thoughts followed them.

We were in Havannah Harbor, Efate, a hot, humid, fetid, disease-ridden, horrible place. It's difficult now to believe such an island existed. We received word the famous hospital ship, USS *Relief* (AH-1) commissioned in 1920, was to arrive with her precious contingent of Navy-nurses.

Unlike the other ships in their various shades of gray, the hospital ships were painted white with a horizontal green stripe and a red cross, beautiful to the color-starved men on the gray Pacific ships and olive drab stations.

On that memorable New Hebrides morning, *Relief* steamed up the channel in her white, green, and red glory. Every bearing gun was trained her way, as were all rangefinders, signal telescopes, and binoculars, as she entered, anchored, then swung to with her rust-streaked, war-weary sisters.

All hands topside spelled one another at the glasses. It had been eight months since we waved good-bye to the girl in white back at Pearl.

And there were the nurses, dressed in white! Appointed assistant shore patrol officer for the day, it was a privilege to assist the young ladies from their boat.

USS *Relief*'s nurses — their smiles, their perfume, their beautiful hair, the utter sweetness of womankind — forever fixed in our minds was that enthralling vision of love-liness.

Fortunate are the men who, for an extended period, are deprived of feminine companionship. Their appreciation of the ladies will probably be enhanced — for all their lives.

The arrival of the hospital ship with the nurses was a welcome break, but there we were, still swinging around the hook, day after day, week after week, in that fascinatingly odious Havannah Harbor.

The ship's company seemed to be divided into two groups: Some just wanted to go home. "Stateside" was in their daily thoughts. Others who, even with a war on, had responded to that old peacetime Navy "pitch" — "Join the Navy and see the world!" wanted to continue West to see that world. Songs like "on the road to Mandalay, where the flying fishes play" teased the imagination. Couldn't we, at least, go on to Australia or New Zealand while we were waiting?

About then, we had a pleasant surprise, which greatly eased the tedium: Suddenly, a huge supply of cigarettes arrived. Every pack bore a printed label: "Greetings from the Associated Students of the University of Maryland." It was a magnificent gesture.

Later, we moved to Espiritu Santo and became ac-quainted with the officers and men of the three-stack heavy cruiser, HMAS *Australia*.

The Australians were a vigorous lot much addicted to violent deck hockey. In many of their contests the junior officers pitched themselves against the enlisted men. The sailors once even had an Aussie officer hanging over the lifeline. His face wore a desperate look as though he was not at all sure they were going to allow his return to the deck. The grinning seamen did relent, but both sides would constantly "miss" the small rope puck with their sticks and connect with the opposition's ankles.

We were to see more of HMAS *Australia* under tragic circumstances.

Some unique experiences helped while away the tedium. One afternoon there was a school of sharks swimming off the stern. We watched for a while and then it was suggested we try to catch one. "You'll be sorry!" said the butcher, but he provided a meat hook and some beef. With the hook attached to a length of chain, baited, and secured to a heavy coil of line, we were soon rigged for the Great Shark Hunt. And we did catch a shark. Not an ordinary shark, either. My mind persists in the production of a twenty-foot image.

We then had a problem as our catch would not relax. He thrashed, clashed and gnashed his teeth, glaring at us.

There was a shout, "Throw him back."

Splendid idea, but we had to remove the hook first.

Some of us jumped on his back to hold him still for a moment. He was tremendously strong, stronger than anything we ever experienced. When we found he could not be quieted, some felt he should be dispatched.

A few of us had knives on our combat belts in case an explosion should blow us into the water with sharks nearby. Horrified, we discovered his hide wouldn't be penetrated with those sharp-pointed weapons.

Finally, our sporting captain, C.H. Jones, USN, who was watching from the bridge, passed the word over the loudspeakers, "Whatever those officers are doing for fun on the quarterdeck, please knock it off."

We carefully approached the monster. He had calmed somewhat, but he was still violently alive. We found handholds somehow, cut the line, and slid our reluctant visitor over the side.

Besides being wet and bruised, we were more than a little ashamed. It was a thoughtless and cruel thing to do.

But our days of idleness would soon end.

4

TARAWA

Tarawa was a bitter lesson for the Allies. A series
of misfortunes dogged the operation — unpredict-
able tides, miscalculations, a terrain that forced
troops to wade in under Japanese fire — resulting in heavy
casualties. Rarely has a small piece of land been as well-
protected or stubbornly defended as was Betio Island.

In the early morning of November 20, 1943, at
Betio Island, Tarawa, *Maryland* engaged a Japanese 8-
inch shore battery and silenced it with our heavy guns.

Our burly "Gun Boss," Commander Bruce Kelley,
USN, USNA, Class of 1925, was under orders to use the
main battery with discretion because, as the flagship of the
Southern Attack Force under Admiral Hill, *Maryland* carried the essential communication equipment. Major caliber gunfire shock could disable tube-equipped radios such
as ours.

But when the Japanese suddenly opened on us, we returned the fire with sufficient main battery force. Evidently the engine exhaust from our observation plane on the catapult provided the aiming point for the Japanese fire control crew. The OS2U, manned by Lieutenant Commander MacPherson and his radioman, Robert C. Houle, ARM 3/c, USNR, was being warmed up in the pre-dawn darkness.

Our subsequent bombardment of the Marine landing areas by the 16-inch and both 5-inch batteries was not as effective as it might have been. We were given areas to cover in precisely designated times with a stipulated number of rounds for each battery of each ship.

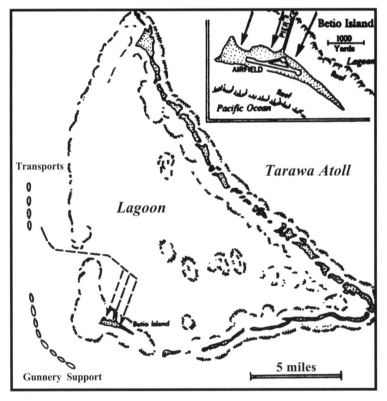

The assault on Tarawa. World War II.

Peering through my glass from our foretop station, all that could be seen of the Betio target areas after a few minutes of firing was a mass of smoke and dust. The tracers on the shells from my guns were disappearing into that great cloud. "Mac, I have no idea where those shells are landing," I reported to the secondary battery commander. Presumably he informed the gunnery officer. Soon there was a tap on my shoulder, "Nothing we can do, Howard, keep shooting."

The sight must have been heartening to the 2nd Division Marines as they approached in their amphibious tractors and in their other landing craft: the blasts and flame from the ships, the spoutings of earth and sand, coconut logs flung high into the air, buildings disintegrating, towering water splashes, the thunderous sounds . . .

Area fire has its uses in the disposition of camouflage, disruption of communications, and the like, but on Betio many of the enemy were inside structures consisting of four feet of concrete with additional layers of coconut logs. All this was covered with sand, giving the appearance of sand dunes.

As soon as we completed our initial bombardment, the surviving defenders quickly manned their shore defenses. An unusually low tide nearly exposed the reef several hundred yards out. Fortunately, the leading Marines were in the amphibious tractors. Some of these were able to cross the reef and reach the beaches against the hostile fire.

This was an agonizing dilemma for Admiral Hill and General Julian Smith, USMC, Marine Division commander. They had tremendous gunfire and aircraft support available, but it could be applied only with the utmost care after the Marines entered the target zones. Bad communications caused additional difficulties.

The situation did not substantially improve for many hours. The first night was a perilous one for the few men ashore in two isolated pockets. They were under the command of Colonel David Shoup, USMC, who had been wounded. He later received the Medal of Honor from President Roosevelt.

The Japanese ship, *Saida Maru*, stranded on the reef, weighed heavily on Colonel Shoup's mind. Japanese snipers and machine gunners had occupied it and were enfilading the troops wading toward the beach. The colonel attempted to silence them with Marine pack howitzers. No luck. Next he called in Navy dive bombers. There were many near-misses, but the Japanese fire continued. The colonel then tried dynamite-laden Marine sappers. Still no luck. *(text continues on p. 57)*

Written in 1994, the following is Robert C. Houle's personal account of his dawn flight over Betio Island with Lt. Cmdr. Robert A. MacPherson, USN:

First Combat . . . Tarawa, Nov. 20, 1943

In that pre-dawn darkness the *Maryland* moved silently off Betio Island. The ship's crew was at battle stations as I sat in the rear seat of our "Kingfisher" scout-observation plane waiting for our catapult launch with some trepidation. It was to be my first taste of combat. My pilot, Lt. Cmdr. MacPherson, flag aviator, was revving the engine and completing his final pre-takeoff check. We noticed a flash of gunfire from Betio Island, and suddenly an unexpected large splash in the water near our ship. After a moment, it suddenly dawned on me, "My God, the Japs are shooting at us!" That prompted return fire from our main battery which silenced the Japanese 8-inch coastal gun. It was quite an experience in that dark pre-dawn hour. We found out later the exhaust flames from the plane's engine made the ship a target and established range.

Finally we were launched. As we approached Betio, at about 1,500 feet, the entire panorama of combat was unveiled in the early morning sunlight. Ships of all sizes and classification were everywhere. On the island, smoke and heavy gunfire indicated the concentration of naval bombardment. Marines were being disgorged from troopships and amphibious landing craft were circling in advance of heading toward designated beaches. The smell of shell explosions soon permeated the confines of our OS2U as we lowered our altitude. That smell later changed to a sickening stench of death.

Robert C. Houle, Aviation Radioman Third Class, USN.

As we flew lower and lower (400 to 500 feet) the activity below grew more intense. As the Marines approached the beaches the Japanese artillery, mortars and machine guns began taking a horrendous toll. Entire boatloads of men could be seen erupting skyward as on-target mortar shells found their mark with deadly accuracy. Survivors made their way toward that murderous firepower in shoulder-deep water with rifles held above their heads. Others sought shelter near a long wooden pier which supported what appeared to be toilets. Nearby was a Japanese ship which apparently was sunk by an earlier attack. But, it was not a refuge. The Japanese had manned it with soldiers and fire power which exacted a heavy toll on the Americans. From the air we could see one area, at least 500 feet in diameter, which was red with Marine blood. We also observed a destroyer which was hung up on a reef, testimony to what was later admitted as faulty tides intelligence.

The sight of the carnage below sickened me. It brought tears to my eyes. And it wasn't from the battle smoke below which we could smell. What I observed I relayed to Lt. Cmdr. MacPherson. He relayed our observations back to command ship *Maryland*. As we flew lower through the haze of battle smoke, I could feel our plane being hit with small arms fire from below. We were at an altitude of only 300 to 400 feet. Suddenly there was a noise in the cockpit, an impact on my back, and a hot pain. I had been hit, and it scared the hell out of me. I was hurt, but I didn't think it was too serious. Fortunately it wasn't. Even so, I was aware there were more bullets coming at us and I could hear and feel the impacts on our "Kingfisher." I informed Mr. MacPherson I had been wounded and we curtailed our flight and returned to the ship.

Strangely, a song we had been listening to in our aviation workshop the night before kept going 'round and 'round in my head after I was hit. It was "Street of Dreams" by Tommy Dorsey with Frank Sinatra on the vocal. Damn strange!

In returning to the ship, Mr. MacPherson made a good landing and taxied to the ship. As usual, I got on the wing, waited for the ship's crane hook to be lowered and attached it to the hoisting sling behind the pilot. As we were being raised to the quarterdeck I could see the recovery crew reacting to the numerous holes in our float which was discharging streams of water resembling a garden sprinkler. This scene was repeated several more times as Mr. MacPherson wore out three aircraft in his forays over the battle-torn island. He was a hell of a man! He was awarded a Silver Star for his valiant efforts at Betio, Tarawa. He deserved more.

After getting my wound treated and bandaged, the Lt. Cmdr. and I went up to the flag bridge to report to Admiral Harry Hill and General Julian Smith. After Mr. MacPherson gave his report I returned to our aviation workshop and sacked out on the deck. Huh, big deal getting wounded and becoming the first *Maryland* casualty since Pearl Harbor. But this was only the beginning. There was a lot more war ahead.

(continued from page 54)

Finally, reluctantly, because of the risk to the troops from a wild shot, he requested heavy gunfire from *Maryland* and *Colorado*.

Our 16-inch obliterated the target, and we killed no Marines.

The Pearl Harbor veterans, especially, and we others, too, were much cheered by this first strike in retribution against the Japanese. Japanese 8-inch guns opened the battle of Tarawa firing the first shot at the USS *Maryland*. The Japanese batteries then turned to open fire on the transports just north of the entrance to the lagoon. These guns were taken under fire by the USS *Maryland,* which silenced them after two salvos. The *Maryland* then moved in to approximately 2,300 yards and enfiladed Green Beach 1 and 2 down to the other battery on the northwest point for a period of three hours. On D-Day Plus One the USS *Santa Fe* methodically ripped the same area to pieces from an average range of about 3,000 yards using slow fire and working from north to south for a period of two

Gansevoort, Meade *and* Frazier *were all Benson Class destroyers. Pictured is a sister,* Livermore. *U.S. Navy.*

The Japanese submarine I-15, *here shown on trials, was a sister to the* I-35. *Conway Picture Library Collection.*

hours. These 8-inch guns were of British manufacture and possibly moved to this site from Singapore.

A sign giving *Maryland* full credit was later erected before the ruins of that shore battery.

On November 22nd the fleet standing by off Tarawa was attacked by a Japanese submarine.

Destroyer USS *Gansevoort* (DD-608) made the first contact and attacked with accurate depth charges. Sister ships, USS *Meade* (DD-602) and USS *Frazier* (DD-607), soon moved in to assist. *I-35*, commanded by Lieutenant Commander Yamamoto, was forced to the surface and then was attacked by strafing aircraft and ships' gunfire. There was a jet of black smoke from *Frazier* as she came up to speed. She heeled over in a sharp turn and at fifteen knots her skipper drove that sharp bow right amidships into the submarine. *I-35* immediately sank with all hands except two or three, whom the destroyers rescued, treated, and transferred. The damaged *Frazier*, commanded by Cdr. E.M. Brown, USN, then departed.

Tarawa was secured as a heavy cost; over 1,000 Marines and sailors killed; over 2,000 wounded. But the hard lessons learned were the foundation for victory in the amphibeous operations to come.

5

HOME FOR
CHRISTMAS

One of the world's finest experiences is to steam up the San Francisco Main Ship Channel toward the Golden Gate Bridge on a fog-free early morning. The sun rises sharply over the East Bay hills, and that magnificent bridge grows from a colorful child's toy in the far distance to a huge, graceful structure which dwarfs our suddenly insignificant battleship as we slip quietly underneath. All those months in the Pacific had exacted a severe toll on our hull, electronics, guns and machinery. The Pearl Harbor Navy Yard was full, so we were awarded an availability at the relatively new Hunters Point Naval Shipyard in San Francisco.

Plowing along the waterfront, our thoughts turned from the sea to families, homes, and Christmas.

Passing beneath the west span of the San Francisco-Oakland Bay Bridge in 1936, Maryland *presents the same aspect as seen from the Golden Gate bridge in 1944. Note "46" on turret No. 2. The heavy black fore and aft lines across the forepart of the ship are probably the work of a military censor during World War II. Naval Historical Center.*

It was a glorious Christmas at home in Fort Bragg, a small lumber and fishing town by the sea in Northern California. Many of Fort Bragg's young men grew up around boats. It was only natural that quite a few chose the Navy when the country needed them.

Leaves were brief, and soon all the ship's company was back on board *Maryland* preparing for the forthcoming operations.

We quickly fell back into the daily cycle of life at sea. Of greatest importance was our ongoing training for surface action against the Japanese battle force. Nineteen forty-four would be the peak of the war on both ocean fronts. In the Pacific, the hard core of the Japanese Navy remained afloat and our duty was to meet and defeat the heavy ships of their battle line.

New, fast battleships such as the *Iowa, Missouri, New Jersey* and *Wisconsin* were being delivered rapidly to the Pacific theater. Many aviators felt the aircraft from the carriers would relegate all new and old battleships to support and bombardment roles. Still, we had no thought of turning in our armor-piercing shell allowance of thirty rounds per main battery gun. They were always ready on the shell decks.

The turret crews and the main battery fire control people continued to hone the techniques developed through years of practice. The secondary battery drilled constantly in the protection of the ship against enemy destroyer, submarine, and aircraft torpedo attack, and our antiaircraft batteries worked steadily at the improvement of their marksmanship.

Most naval personnel have heard the question: "In all those peacetime years, and during all those months in war between operations, what do you do with no live targets at which to shoot?"

A fair answer could never be brief: There isn't enough time to do all we should be doing. In a well-run ship there is something going on almost constantly, underway and in port; in war and in peace. For example:

General quarters, drills for every emergency, quarters for muster, divine services, watch standing, loading drill.

Target practice, engineering sea trials, aircraft operations.

Fueling at sea and in port, loading stores and ammunition.

Rig for towing (we once completely rigged to tow *Colorado*. Admiral Hill decided not to get her moving, much to our disappointment.)

Gunnery and engineering struggles for the peacetime "E."[1]

Landing force organization and training (we carried a field artillery piece, rifles, and other small arms.)

Captain's weekly inspection.

Discipline, including Captain's Mast, Deck Courts Martial, and Summary Courts Martial.

Repair and maintenance, hull reports (weekly inspections by junior officers of every compartment for watertight integrity).

Classes, study, examinations for promotion (nearly all hands).

Temporary additional duty training at shore schools.

Conferences of all officers in the wardroom.

---

[1] High level performance to various standards earns U.S. Navy warships the right to paint an "E" for excellence on their superstructure.

Ceremonies for visiting officials, official visits ashore in foreign ports, escorting visitors about the ship, visits to foreign naval vessels.

Physical exercises, daily, sports, handicrafts, movies, smokers.

And:

Correspondence
Machinery histories (originated by Fleet Admiral King)
Planning for naval yard availabilities
Rough and smooth deck logs
Action reports
Decoding and encoding messages
Corrections to classified publications
Nautical chart corrections
Personnel accounting
Censoring (every day in wartime). . . .

Not everyone had to do all the above, of course, but, if you ever wanted a command, no matter how small, you had better know how to do it all, and know when it's not done, or not done right.

The key to getting all the work properly done is the executive officer. He navigates in a smaller vessel, and in all ships, large or small, he corrects the mistakes and omissions of each department so the captain doesn't begin to feel he is commanding a sea-going turkey farm.

Maryland's quiet efficiency was always impressive.

Much of this can be attributed to the executive officer who gave us a fine start at the war's beginning. Commander R.H. Hillenkoeter, USN, USNA, class of 1919, qualified in submarines. He served in destroyers, a cruiser, and was *Maryland*'s gunnery officer in 1937. He was

West Virginia's executive officer and was wounded during the Battle of Pearl Harbor.   With that ship sunk, he became *Maryland*'s exec.   Later, he commanded destroyer tender *Dixie* in the Solomons, and was awarded the Bronze Star.   He commanded the famous new battleship USS *Missouri*, (BB-63), after the war's end.   Ashore, he taught modern language at the Naval Academy, was naval attaché at the American Embassy in Paris, and earlier assisted in the procurement of the Swiss Oerlikon 20-mm antiaircraft gun for use in all the ships of the American Navy.

Later, as an admiral, this illustrious, exceptionally versatile officer was director of the Central Intelligence Group from 1947 to 1950.   This and the OSS [Office of Strategic Services] were the forerunners of the present Central Intelligence Agency.   Vice Admiral Hillenkoeter's last active duty service was as the Navy's Inspector General in 1956.

Vice Admiral R.H. Hillenkoeter, USN, who, as a commander, was executive officer of Maryland *from December 15, 1941 to July 3, 1942.   U.S. Navy.*

6

KWAJALEIN

At Kwajalein, the Navy put into practice the lessons of Tarawa beginning with a prolonged and thorough bombardment. On January 30, 1944, USS *Maryland*, in company with cruisers *Indianapolis*, *Santa Fe* and *Biloxi*, opened fire on Roi Island, the northernmost of the many islands which comprised Kwajalein Atoll in the Marshalls.

Kwajalein lies in the center of the Pacific, south of Wake Island, and had been under Japanese mandate from the League of Nations since 1920. Roi and its twin, Namur, contained a major air base, seaplane anchorage, and submarine facilities.

A question for many years was: Had the Japanese fortified the Marshalls and Carolines in defiance of their mandate's provisions?

The cruiser Indianapolis *as she appeared in July, 1945. U.S. Navy.*

At Tarawa, our efforts were not completely effective. Many Japanese survived our bombardment in their blockhouses and pillboxes. The staffs pored over the results and refined techniques for the Marshalls campaign. With information from submarine periscope and air photographs, relief models of the target islands were constructed. Miniatures of each blockhouse, pillbox, and gun emplacement were secured to the models and each given a code name. All ships and batteries were assigned targets, and the battery officers familiarized themselves with the names, features, and locations.

At Roi Island we first fired general area coverage with high capacity shells, most of which were fitted with contact fuses. This disposed of the camouflage, destroyed most communications, and wrecked other unprotected equipment. Aircraft bombing, of course, complemented this phase. The preliminary shelling was done at longer range to produce plunging fire and to minimize ricochets from the flat surface.

We then closed the range — 2,000 to 1,000 yards — just "down the block" for the main battery. Our commander, Vice Admiral Richard Conolly, USN, had earned the nickname "Close-in-Conolly" for his close gunfire support during the Sicily invasions and at Salerno.

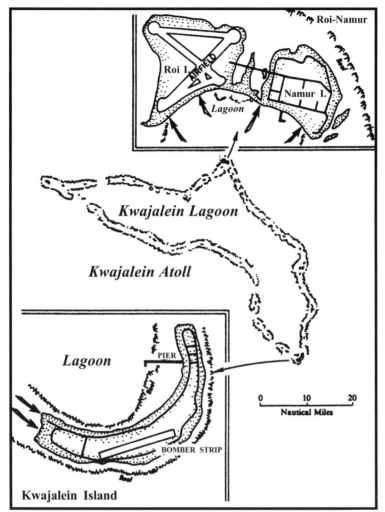

The assault on Kwajalein Atoll. World War II.

The Turret III guns were "loaded and laid." The all-important pointer, his crosswires precisely on target, closed his firing key. The two huge shells were on their way through the massive gun barrels recoiling just over his head. The trajectory was almost flat, and probably two salvos would be required.

In the foretop we followed the shells in through our glasses, although it's possible to see those 16-inchers in flight with the unaided eye. We saw a pair hit at the blockhouse's base, and two round holes appeared dead center. As one shell detonated, the structure's top immediately erupted in a vast geyser of flame, smoke, and debris. Many believed they saw the second shell explode on the runway behind, which meant it had actually penetrated both walls before the fuse functioned. The projectiles passed through at least four feet of concrete — maybe more — and accounted for all those within.

Later, while spotting our own 5-inch gunfire, I sighted an incoming 14-inch or 16-inch shell in my glass. By its wobble it could be recognized as a ricochet off the island from a battleship firing from the opposite side.

We were steaming ahead and away — fortunately — and it quickly became evident the spent projectile was going to fall short and astern.

"Watch where I'm pointing!" I shouted, indicating a spot in the ocean.

Everyone looked in time to see a great spout of water rise to nearly foretop level.

Despite heavy damage and casualties, the Japanese continued to resist and the island had to be taken inch by inch, man by man. Soon after, the islands were secured with relatively small American loss of life — 372 casualties out of 41,000 troops. The Japanese lost 7,870 men out of 8,675.

A group of *Maryland*'s gunnery officers and chief petty officers was invited ashore to inspect our bombardment results. The Marines treated us well, as *Maryland* was understandably a heroine to them. They were members of the 4th Marine Division commanded by Major General Harry "Hardnails" Schmidt, USMC.

*Results of battleship, cruiser and destroyer gunfire, Marshall Islands,
1944.   E.W. Fredell.*

Inside Blockhouse "Bruce," there were dozens, hundreds, of dead. No one stayed to count. We searched for our 5-inch fire effects. In the general destruction, we could not be sure which battery did what, but we did find one of our shell nose plugs embedded in a gun site parapet. As we examined the fortifications, they appeared weather-beaten, older than the three years which had elapsed since the war's beginning.

Turret III's Chief Turret Captain W. F. McGraw, USN, had been in naval service for thirty years, and at fifty-two was an acknowledged authority on main battery gunnery. He was a dedicated instructor of officers and enlisted men, and he took tremendous pride in his work. His carefully maintained guns had demolished blockhouse "Bruce," and when he completed his tour of Roi Island, he said: "If I die tomorrow, I'll die happy!"

Upon his return to the ship, he praised the pointer and trainer, the sightsetter, and his loading crews, who all had performed so well. The chiefs sat up late in the CPO mess discussing the great day and then turned in.

Discharging 5-inch ammunition the hard way prior to departure for the United States to regun the 16-inch main battery after the Marshalls campaign, 1944.   Author.

Chief McGraw passed away about 0330 the next morning . . .

The official Navy report of *Maryland*'s performance at Roi Island reads:

ACCURATE AND EFFECTIVE, HAVING ACHIEVED THE SUCCESSFUL DESTRUCTION OF THE ENEMY'S ORGANIZED DEFENSE.

We were all in high spirits, and most felt even better after a complete inspection of a Turret I gun. The main battery gunners suspected something amiss as the gun's liner slightly protruded. With the muzzle lowered nearly to the deck, the slim turret officer climbed in. The gun was elevated. He slid out of sight on a line and with a flashlight. This is not done every day, so the attention was widespread.

"If he gets stuck, can we shoot him out?"

"He's in a good spot in case of an air raid."

"What will he do, if we get sunk?"

"Glub!"

Lieutenant (jg) J. B. Thro, USN, USNA, Class of 1941, was all business when he finally reappeared, but then he saw the sea of expectant faces. Imagine a crowd of young sailors, joking and laughing in the sun. Then picture that officer, his head and shoulders slowly emerging from the giant rifle, his blackened, sweat-streaked face suddenly lighting with a wry grin.

"It's broken!" The gun liner had split due to the intense firing.

There was a round of cheers. Everyone knew the shipyard specializing in the re-gunning of battleship main batteries was located at Bremerton, Washington, U.S.A.!

We soon anchored in the lagoon and received aboard Admiral Conolly with his staff. We served as flagship and storeship for about two weeks, during which we had one air raid with no damage to us.

Maryland and her company had shaken down into a cohesive operating unit. There was more work to be done, but we knew she could do it, and she could do it well. We were one proud crew.

Captain Ray was in command as we headed east for new guns.

This type of weather did little to dampen our spirits as we headed toward the United States. Author.

7

TORPEDOED AT SAIPAN

W e re-gunned at Bremerton, then headed for another operation — no idea where. Westward
Ho! Our old iron charger was loaded. We had
our fun, so it was up and away. Seattle, good-bye.

When the bow begins to lift to those long ocean
swells and you breathe the clean air, you think how small
is your vessel upon the vastness of the great ocean. At sea
we move in the center of a constant circle of water and
hemisphere of sky. Everything in this capsule is constantly moving and changing — clouds, the colors of the
sea; the sun, moon, planets, and stars, journeying across
the sky in their precise and predictable paths. The mainland has descended behind the horizon astern, and, until an
island emerges over the horizon ahead, we and our escort
are alone with the eternal verities.

There is always 0800 quarters for muster unless in action, or if, for some other reason, the executive officer tells the officer of the deck to pass the happy word: "Now, muster on stations. Turn in all reports to the executive officer's office." The captain and the executive officer are, of course, responsible for all on board. They must always know that everyone is present or accounted for. At sea, especially, a man could go overboard, or be lying unconscious, or dead, in some remote part of the ship.

Next morning came the call: "Now, all hands fall in to quarters for muster." The sky was gray, dripping with cold, dreary fog. The ship was quietly quartering the swells, which gave her that combination heave and roll so disconcerting to those on their first trip. The long lines of men in the Fifth Division, dressed in work clothes with their regular white hats dyed blue, were all in "automatic mode."

As *Maryland* rolled down to starboard, they individually swayed to port, in perfect alignment. As the bow went down, they swayed aft in unison. The ship's motion was heavy, though not violent. Not a single sailor broke ranks as they stood, steady in space, part of the moving ship. It was a fascinating sight.

"All present or accounted for, Sir." This from our new leading petty officer, Gun 4 captain, and "plank owner,"[1] Holderlein, BM1/c. He helped put *Maryland* in commission and had served aboard since. His report was accompanied with a quick, friendly gesture you could call a salute, which I returned. It was about the only formal military display all day long between officers and men aboard our ship in wartime.

---

[1] A "plank owner" is someone who was on board a ship when it was commissioned.

THE PETTY OFFICER

Movie and television actors seldom portray that sea-going salute accurately. Let me try to explain the relationship between officer and petty officer as it develops and how it then gives meaning to this casual greeting: Division leading petty officers aboard ship have status and functions similar to those of Army first sergeants. The division officer transacts most of the official division business through him, and, if that officer is fortunate, the leading PO takes care of most of the routine personnel problems. A good one, of course, consults regularly with the division head.

"That new kid on Gun 8 catches on quick. Do you need a sharp talker in the tops?" Or, "The first shellman on Gun 6 is gone, as you know, but the second shellman is not too hefty. There's two good ones on Gun 2. What do you think about shifting one down there?"

The good leading PO also keeps his division officer generally informed as to what is going on. Are the people upset about something? The chow okay? We reserves learned a great deal about the seafaring life from those old sea dogs.

First Class Boatswain's Mate Holderlein was the third leading petty officer of the Fifth Division since I reported aboard. Promotion and new construction took the first two, and we hated to see them go. We were pleased, however, when the replacements took over without a break in the administration of the one hundred and thirty man division.

The first was Edward E. Cowden, a first class boatswain's mate when I first knew him. An old China hand, he had served in USS *Panay*,[2] the famous gunboat on Yangtze River patrol. When the Japanese sank her in 1937, Chief Cowden, then a coxswain, received the Navy

---

[2] The first American commander of *Panay*, formerly a Spanish ship, was Ensign Chester W. Nimitz, USN, in 1907.

Cross for his rescue of the seriously wounded commanding officer and for his operation of the ship's motor sampan during the aircraft attacks. A copy of Chief Cowden's
official citation is not available, but a copy of the micro-
film record follows:

COWDEN, Edward E., Cox, USN
Between wars 1931 to 1941
Awarded: NAVY CROSS

For distinguishing himself by display of heroism on the occasion of the bombing and loss of the USS PANAY on 12
Dec. 1937. Cowden voluntarily acted as Coxswain of the
motor sampan and made all trips in this boat, thus exposing
himself to many attacks from hostile planes. His excellent
performance of duty, under the most difficult and hazardous
conditions, was in keeping with the highest traditions of the
Naval Service.

When Chief Boatswain's Mate Cowden was pro-
moted, he moved to the chief petty officers' mess and
subsequently to new construction. Boatswain's Mate First
Class Rooney then took over. A powerful, vigorous man
he had no problem maintaining the respect of the division.
He is, in my memory, a career man-o'-warsman in the
traditional mold. Excellent in character and appearance,
he wore his uniform as if it were designed specifically for
the build and looks of such a man as he.

These men — CBM Cowden, BM1/c Rooney, BM1/e
Holderlein, with the guns maintained by such outstanding men as
Chief Gunner's Mate Davidson and Gunner's Mate First Class
Barr — are a few of the thousands of efficient petty officers the
Navy recruited and trained during the peacetime years. Without
them, our wartime Navy likely would have been an expen-
sive and pathetic farce. History reveals navies like that:
all show and no internal strength.

Ships may be built quite rapidly, once the ship-yards get started. Ships may be recommissioned from the reserve fleets in as little as a month. To produce the seamen I've described requires almost a lifetime working at sea.

After receiving Holderlein's report on that foggy morning, I walked aft to the gunnery officers' meeting. Most of the men in the divisions I passed had somber faces. They were thinking, no doubt, of those left behind and of the long sea miles ahead.

The gun boss was brief: "You all know we've lost a lot of men to new construction. Key men, too. We haven't much time until the next operation. I don't want any of the men hurt on the guns, so you all know what it's going to be." He paused and then grinned. "Loading drill, plenty of it. The old hands will gripe. They've been wearing out those loading machines for two and a half years now. Let 'em bellow. We have to break in the new people."

Back to the forecastle, port side. "Loading drill, Holderlein — Dutch," I said. "Dutch" was his nickname, and I, after addressing him in the regular way, tried to indicate how much I liked and respected him by using it. Senior, regular officers sometimes used first names with old friends in the ranks.

The moans of the troops were not suppressed when Holderlein growled: "You starboard-side loading crews: loading drill. You men on the port crews: Stand by where you can hear the word and get up there quick. I'm looking at you gedunk sailors." (Men who were addicted to the ice cream sundaes and other sweets known as "gedunks," sold at the ship's soda fountain. It usually opened right after quarters in the morning and drove some of the leading

POs crazy. I used to tell Holderlein it was a good idea. "You know where to look for your drop-outs.")

Holderlein continued: "You get in that line down there, and you don't want to lose your place when the word is passed. No excuses. Everybody there. We have to get in shape after chasing around Seattle. Did you want to say anything, Mr. Sauer?"

"Yeah," I answered. "We're not going west for our health, as you know. We did okay at Tarawa and in the Marshalls, but there's a lot more to be done. You old hands have proven you can really shoot. The skipper and the gun boss are proud of you. It's too bad we can't sit on our butts and admire the passing scenery. But we have to start all over again with the loading machine. We've a bunch of new men, and we have to learn what they can do. See you on the boat deck!"

Maryland was back at Pearl, right where she was on December 7, 1941, moored in berth "Fox 5." The *Oklahoma* was gone. *Arizona* and her crew lay entombed in the harbor. Again, the scene rekindled the memories of the men who had served on board that tragic Sunday morning.

Bombardment rehearsals were carried out off Maui and Kahoolawe with our new fire support group. Then we sailed for Roi Island in Kwajalein. There, we Marshall Island veterans pointed out the locale of our achievement to the new people. Such is the life of a warship. The officers and men come and go, but the ship remains, and her traditions grow.

The conquest of Saipan, together with Tinian and Guam, was the largest amphibious operation to that time, partly due to the vast distances involved; it was 3,500 miles from Pearl Harbor and a thousand mile "hop" from the nearest advance base at Eniwetok, which was little more than an anchorage. Invading Saipan was also a threat to Japan, which regarded that island as part of the homeland.

Soon after our departure from Roi-Namur we officially learned our destination: Saipan! Inspection of the chart revealed an astounding westward leap. It had two purposes: First, the disrupting of Japan's communication with her southern empire. Second, the Army Air Force B-29 Superfortress was ready for battle. Its operation from China wasn't too satisfactory because of supply problems and Japanese Army encroachment of Chinese air strips. We required a more easily-supplied, secure base with enough land room for several good-sized runways and support facilities.

The chart showed the best areas to be Saipan, Tinian, and Guam.

At quarters the first morning at sea, Holderlein again invited me to talk to the division.

"You've probably already heard we're going to Saipan," I said. "It's a big operation with air cover from fifteen or twenty carriers. It's amazing. A couple of years ago the only operating fleet carrier in the Pacific was the *Enterprise*. Back aft, they think the Japanese Fleet could come out. If they do, we have our whole fleet along, beside the carriers. We have about seven new battleships, plus our old ones, and there's plenty of cruisers and destroyers. Admiral Spruance is in charge, and you know he did real well at Midway.

"The fly boys are going to hit Saipan first, and then the new battleships will bombard.

"Talking about the new battleships: One of the people in the tops asked me awhile back if the big new ones — *Iowa* and *New Jersey* — had elevators to their foretops. I checked. They don't. Their people have to climb, just like us. They're fine ships, though — big! We may get to see 'em. Long bows, lots of sheer, nine guns in three turrets, like the *North Carolina* we saw in San Francisco, back in June of '42. The main thing about them is that they are fast, a lot faster than even the *South Dakota*.

"Back to business. After the new ships fire, then we are going in, and they're going to give us plenty of time to shoot, like at Roi-Namur, and not at Tarawa. It's something we can do better than the new ships, because we've had more practice."

The new battleships and our first-line carrier-based aircraft went in on schedule. We then began our bombardment on June 14, 1944. It was deliberate, carefully spotted fire, and it was effective as far as it went. We had solved the blockhouse problem in the Marshalls, but we found we would never be without a challenge. This time it was caves, and it was Corregidor all over again, with the roles reversed.[3]

More rough work for the Marine and Army infantry.

By then we had organized and trained shore fire control parties in the front lines. Probably the most effective role for the gunfire support group was to respond to specific requests by direct radio from the shore teams for fire on a designated target. The ship assigned, which stood by hour after hour, day and night, actually was transformed into a sea-going heavy artillery battery. (The Navy performed this function in World War I with railway-car-mounted 14-inch naval rifles.)

---

[3] Corregidor, a rocky, fortified island at the entrance to Manila Bay, contained an extensive network of protective tunnels. It was considered impossible to win control of the island through heavy bombardment. The Japanese couldn't do it in 1942, and, later, neither could the Americans.

We also answered requests for illumination by star shell, and we did some interdiction fire. The latter consisted usually of one-gun salvos continuously fired at odd intervals on road or trail intersections, on narrow canyon roads, or on cave entrances. Its purpose was to interfere with enemy movements.

If we set out to design a ship for that work today, the result would still be something like *Maryland*. Her heavy guns, armor with extensive compartmentation, seakeeping ability, and her great endurance were all essential. We did need more speed and a dual purpose secondary battery. (*Maryland* received that battery in 1945.)

The *Iowa* class battleships are the fastest ever built. In addition to standard armament, they also have long-range missiles of astounding accuracy and effective missile defense batteries. We are fortunate they were never dismantled.[4]

One day, off Saipan, our port secondary battery was firing area coverage on Garapan Town, for which the ships had received the famous order to "bomb, shell, and destroy." A pretty village with a few houses showing among the trees, it was proving a difficult obstacle to the Marines. We were firing directly over a small island named Maniagassa.

---

[4] USS *Wisconsin* (BB-64) and USS *Missouri* (BB-63), both of the *Iowa* class, demonstrated their worth in the 1990-91 Persian Gulf War. Their Tomahawk missiles and 16-inch and 5-inch gunfire contributed to the "softening-up" process. That heavy gunfire support would have been welcome had a Marine landing operation been required. Not to be forgotten: the heartening effect of the great ships in sight of the attacking Marines and the defenders' disheartening reaction to those huge shells! (Ask any Guadalcanal Marine veteran his memories of the Japanese battleship bombardment in 1942 — and they were 14-inchers!)

Full broadside from main battery of USS New Jersey. *Note shunt to port. U.S. Navy.*

Suddenly, I saw in the bottom of my binocular field gun flashes from that island. They were not firing on us, but at *Tennessee* or *California*, to the south. Both ships had been hit, earlier in the operation, by shore gun fire.

"Check fire, check fire; shifting targets!" I sent over my phone to the gun captains. There was no time to get a range from sky control, but I had seen the chart and now estimated that Maniagassa Island lay about one-and-a-half miles toward us from Garapan. (It was actually more than that, but, somehow, our shells landed just about right.)

"On target!" reported the director pointer.

"In 3,000!" from me to BM2/c Kichli, USNR, the rangekeeper operator. He spun his crank, the sightsetter reset his sights, sent his new readings down to the guns, and the director was back in business.

"Counterbattery fire; rapid fire! Resume fire! Resume fire!" I sent down to the director buzzerman and over the telephone to the gun captains.

"Crack!" "Crack!" "Crack!" We hammered them out. Watching our shells speeding away, continuing gun flashes could be seen on the island. They looked larger than 3-inch, but smaller than 8-inch; probably 4.7-inch or 6-inch.

We were short, but right on in bearing, so I spotted out a little and told Kichli: "Rock it!"

This meant to fire one salvo on range, one 200 yards more, one again on range, the next, 200 yards less, then back on range, and repeat.

The range is usually changing with the movement of the ship, but the rangekeeper automatically handles this. The busy Kichli did have to keep the set-up current (the Mark VII rangekeeper required constant manual input of ship's speed). Therefore, "rocking it" as we were, and staying on in bearing, the odds should, sooner or later, give us a hit.

Meanwhile, alerted by our fusillade, and by the secondary battery officer's telephoned report, the main battery swung majestically out to port. The other ships'

USS South Dakota. *National Archives.*

batteries joined the action. We'll never know if *our* 5-inch hit, but we were certain we fired the first of hundreds of rounds which immediately blasted that small island.

Later, on Tinian, a Japanese gun, or guns, in a cave caught our sister ship, *Colorado*, in a similar situation. My first ship received twenty-two direct hits, suffered one hundred and five men killed, and many wounded, all in a few minutes.

In our case, we were fortunate to have our battery in action when the Japanese gun opened. We were even more fortunate my glass happened to be trained on that shore gun site. From then on it was merely automatic. We had drilled for counterbattery fire countless times since May of 1942, and earlier.

The Japanese Combined Fleet did sortie during the Saipan invasion, so we had many air raid alerts. We could see Japanese aircraft on the horizon, burning and falling. This was the celebrated "Marianas Turkey Shoot." The aviators from our carriers shot down some 400 Japanese before most of them could attack our ships, and they sank a Japanese carrier. Our submarines sank two other carriers. *South Dakota* received a bomb hit and there was minor damage to two other American ships.

USS Pennsylvania. *National Archives.*

Maryland's turn was at hand. On June 22nd, the ships anchored for the night. *Pennsylvania* lay a short distance to port. Suddenly, an aircraft crossed her bow and passed us low overhead. We could see its exhaust and its dark shape against the starlight — two engine job, not ours.

A torpedo against the bow! Old *Maryland* shuddered. Her bow heaved up and then down like the head of a beaten horse.

We went to general quarters, but for what? The plane was long gone.

From the enemy's standpoint, that was a beautiful piece of work. It was a dark, but not black, night. They must have come in right on the surface to avoid radar, or they flew in behind Saipan's radar shadow, flipped down to the water, jumped over *Pennsylvania*, dropped their torpedo, hauled back over us, then down and away. The pilot had to have fantastic night vision and incredibly quick reflexes. Perhaps he had studied our positions from Tinian Island, close by, after we anchored and before dark. Then

Burial at sea after Saipan torpedo hit, 1944. Author.

they rolled out their concealed aircraft and quickly made their attack.

The torpedo launched by the mysterious plane from nowhere blew a forty-foot hole all the way through our bow. An aviation fuel tank was ruptured and we could smell the fumes. Fortunately, there was no fire.

The explosion killed two men from our division who were in the forecastle at the time. Because we faced a long, slow passage to Pearl Harbor for repairs, and there were no facilities for preserving the bodies, both were buried at sea.

They lay on two stretchers on the quarterdeck covered by their own national ensigns and attended by their closest shipmates. The engines were stopped. The chaplain, Cdr. C.M. Sitler, USN, read the moving burial-at-sea service. They slid from under the colors, saluted by three rifle volleys from a Marine squad, and then "Taps" by the ship's bugler.

"All engines ahead one-third; two-block the steaming colors."

Then, it was back to Pearl Harbor for repairs to the bow.

Taken in 1926, this view of the Maryland *in dry dock shows her massive size and is much the way her hull would have appeared after torpedo damage in 1944 was repaired. Naval Historical Center.*

Rear Admiral T.D. Ruddock, USN, succeeded Admiral Hill as COMBATDIV 4. After we took the torpedo, Admiral Ruddock left us by breeches buoy to a destroyer and on to *Colorado*. He and his staff did not find it dull there, either.

A forward section replacement was built in the Pearl Harbor Naval Shipyard dry dock. The graceful bow was cut away, trimmed, and stowed at the dock's far end. With the new section in, two cranes lifted our old bow and gently set it back in place. We were pleased to see the perfect fit. True artists in steel, the work the shipyard workers could do with their cranes, cutting torches, and welding equipment was miraculous.

In the summer of 1944 there was a high-level conference at Pearl Harbor. Led by President Roosevelt, it was attended by General MacArthur, Admirals King and Nimitz and others. Their purpose was to decide whether or not to bypass the Philippines.

The president came by, but didn't come aboard *Maryland*. We could see his warm smile, the celebrated up-tipped cigarette holder held between his teeth. He looked over the repair work from his car and waved to us. It was great to see one of the two great leaders of the Western World.

8

PELELIU

August 1944. We finally arrived in the Solomon Islands, locale of the great 1942-43 sea battles. Passing through "Iron Bottom Sound," where many American and Japanese ships were sunk, we thought of those men and their dramatic clashes — visualizing ship against ship at point-blank range, gun batteries flaming in the night; the bombardments, the air actions, the sudden explosions of unexpected torpedoes. This was the months-long struggle for the control of Guadalcanal. We poured in ships, aircraft, and men until the Japanese were overwhelmed.

There was silence as we traversed the area in the bright sunshine, a breeze crossing the water and blowing into the shattered groves of palm trees. The Japanese menace had swelled to this point, then receded.

Allied Forces across the Pacific. World War II

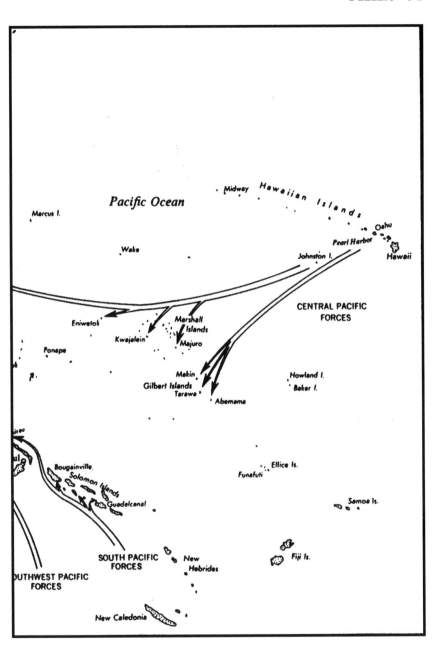

Marcus I.

Pacific Ocean

Midway

Hawaiian Islands

Oahu

Wake

Pearl Harbor

Johnston I.

Hawaii

CENTRAL PACIFIC
FORCES

Eniwetok

Marshall
Islands

Kwajalein

Majuro

Ponape

Makin

Howland I.

Gilbert Islands

Baker I.

Tarawa

Abemama

Ellice Is.

Bougainville

Funafuti

Solomon Islands

Samoa Is.

Guadalcanal

SOUTH PACIFIC
FORCES

New
Hebrides

Fiji Is.

SOUTHWEST PACIFIC
FORCES

New Caledonia

Now we were ordered to the Palaus. Peleliu Island was necessary as an advanced base and the attack on Peleliu Island was underway. Dug into a series of interlocking caves, the Japanese fiercely defended the island, at a high cost in American lives. The landing force was the 1st Marine Division, veterans of Guadalcanal.

There appeared to be a scarcity of targets during our early bombardment. In fact, our commander sent the following message:

> At nightfall there were no more targets on Peleliu worthy of fire. All destroyed. Have ordered bombardment to cease. Await arrival of transports.

Colonel "Chesty" Puller, USMC, commander of the First Marines (regiment), reported during the night after the landing:

> Enemy well dug in. Opposition strong. Little damage done by our preliminary fire (ship bombardment). Casualties over 20 per cent . . .

Here was one more indication of how it would go in later operations such as Iwo Jima and Okinawa. The Japanese were in caves, well-concealed pillboxes, and hidden blockhouses. Not much could be seen from the ships as these defenders awaited the Marines.

Burke Davis in his biography *Marine! The Life of Chesty Puller*, mentioned one blockhouse which was holding up the advance. All within were killed by a direct hit from our ships' big guns.

Colonel Puller's regiment suffered fifty-six per cent casualties in the Peleliu engagement, the highest until then in Marine Corps history. But they eliminated a major blockhouse and 144 caves and pillboxes.

(text continues on p. 96)

Robert C. Houle, who was wounded in that early-morning flight over Betio Island, Tarawa, recounts his experience as radioman with naval aviator Lieutenant Freeman A. Flynn, USNR, in a gunfire spotting mission over Pelelieu Island:

Here we were at another island, Peleliu in the Palau group. We understood it was to be a "piece of cake." Even the Underwater Demolition Team frogmen thought it would be when they posted a sign on one of the beaches after clearing obstacles. The sign read, "Welcome Marines." So it was when the *Maryland* launched aircraft, "Kingfishers," to spot gunfire for what appeared to be a routine bombardment prior to landings by the Marines.

D-day, the actual landing, was scheduled for the morning of September 15, 1944. However, air strikes and naval bombardment began on September 12 to soften the Japanese resistance. The intense shelling and bombing appeared to achieve the desired effect. Even Admiral Oldendorf was mistakenly pleased with his three days of bombardment. He unfortunately reported to Admiral Fort of the amphibious command ship, "We have run out of targets." He did not! But when the vegetation was blown away a new military obstacle was revealed. It was identified as Umurbrogol Ridge, later to become known as "Bloody Nose Ridge," a deadly killing field. It was honeycombed with tunnels and caverns hiding the bulk of an estimated 5,000 Japanese combat troops, weapons and ammunition. Naval bombardment and intense air strikes had little effect on this hidden fortress.

It was on September 12 that Freeman A. Flynn, my pilot, and I were assigned gunfire spotting duties for our ship, the USS *Maryland*. Our targets were in the area of the airfield beneath "Bloody Nose Ridge." We could see enemy gunfire below us and so reported to the *Maryland*. As I leaned over the starboard side of my rear seat position I could even see orange colored tracers coming up at us marking a pattern for antiaircraft shells. Positioning for a better view I turned to the port side of the cockpit. In that instant there was an explosion and shrapnel flew around me. I felt a pain in my right leg and the plane seemed to fall out of control in a downward plunge. Sensing that Mr. Flynn was probably injured and incapacitated I grabbed the emergency control stick from its stowage and seated it. Seeing we were losing altitude I pulled back on the stick and started to head toward the water where our ship was located. In seconds, but what seemed like endless minutes, Mr. Flynn firmly wiggled his control stick indicating he was O.K. The shell that hit us had knocked out our radio. So, our only other communication was a small shuttle tube that we could crank back and forth with written messages. I quickly scribbled a note indicating I had been hit in the leg, but with no profuse bleeding. I then took out a first aid kit, poured some sulfa on the wound and applied a bandage. Next, after frantically patching up the radio gear, we were able to contact the ship.

We flew around at a safe distance from enemy gun-fire and soon Lt. Fred Whaley, our senior aviator, came flying near and below us. He was able to explain where our damage was and the extent. His information revealed we had sustained a large hole in our main float aft of the step. The float had a bottom contour that was configured at two levels. The forward half is deeper than the after section and the forward section is referred to as the step. Landing the plane and settling down on the after portion with the large hole would mean disaster. So, Mr. Flynn asked me if I wanted to hit the silk (parachute) or try a landing. Thinking of my bleeding leg and observing these were shark-filled waters I quickly opted to "go back the same way I got up here."

The ship was notified that we would attempt a landing. It began to position for our approach, and the recovery crew was readied. Now it was up to Mr. Flynn. How good a pilot was he? Had he ever trained for this kind of contingency? Well, he was up to the challenge. We came in hot. We didn't touch down until we were much nearer to the sled and net than we usually were. As soon as we hooked onto the net I jumped out on the wing, grabbed the stern crane hook and attached it to the hoisting sling behind the pilot's seat. This done, I attached the lines leading back to the ship so the crew could control the plane and guide it to the stowage cradle. As the crane raised the plane from the water we heard a big SLURP sound. The plane had been sinking.

It was done, and we were home safe. Mr. Flynn had pulled off one hell of a landing. Once the plane was secured, I climbed down the ladder which the crew provided. Then the ship's doctor examined my leg and asked where I got the bandage. I told him it came from the first aid kit in my cockpit. "Oh," he grunted.

I did a lot of thinking after that. "Somebody up there is watching over me," I mused. "First a bullet in the back at Tarawa; now, turning to the other side of the cockpit that morning just before the antiaircraft shell exploded beneath me and damaged the starboard side. And I thought, this island operation was expected to be a "piece of cake". . . September 12 to November 25: 3,946 1st Marine Division casualties in the first week and thousands of Japanese dead.

Lt. Freeman Flynn:

With that big hole in the main float, there was a question whether the thing would hold together when we hit the water. Bob and I talked it over. I was in favor of jumping out. He was bleeding and a little worried about sharks! So we put it down as close to the ship as we could, bounced once and onto the sled.

> Reported to Captain Ray, as we always did after a combat flight. Sitting in his big chair on the bridge, he looked up (he was a little man), saw that Bob Houle was okay, then made this comment: "Why don't you boys come back as fast as that all the time?"

(continued from p. 92)

After Peleliu we steamed to Manus Island's Seeadler Harbor in the Admiralties. There we joined the Seventh Fleet ships under Admiral Thomas C. Kinkaid, USN, assembled for the Philippines invasion.

This promised to be a difficult operation.

Tarawa was a great shock to many, in and out of the Navy. The battleships, cruisers, and destroyers laid down a tremendous barrage, but when it lifted, the Japanese were still there. We did better in the Marshalls. We improved somewhat at Saipan. We learned more at Peleliu.

USS Maryland's *Turret II fires its 16-inch guns during the bombardment of Peleliu. Author.*

SHORE BOMBARDMENT PROBLEM

The accompanying diagrams will give an idea of the problems encountered — the smoke and dust, the necessity for offset fire, how the offset values change as the ship moves ahead. (Top diagram) Lieutenant McNaughton's "iswas" was adequate on level island targets, but something additional was required when we were presented with the elevated gun emplacements and caves of Saipan. (Middle diagram)

The range is increased on a surface firing naval rifle by elevating the barrel. The rangekeeper and director do this automatically. We are only required to enter the correct range. Now, if we are pointing the director at a surface aiming point, we must enter a third correction for the difference in the target's elevation, as shown. This correction varies as the target's range changes.

The opening salvo is always of great interest to the captain and to the gunnery officer. It is the moment when the fire control officer down in main battery plot, the battery officers on the 5-inch, and all their assistants have the opportunity to display their abilities. Corrections for air and powder temperatures have been entered. The ship's course and speed are in (automatic in the newer equipment). True wind course and speed have been cranked in. There is a gun-wear correction and one arising from the earth's rotation. An especially interesting one is the cold-gun correction, entered for the first salvo, and then removed. Much has been written about that one, but essentially it is a "Jesus factor." Its direction and amount depends on the fire control officer's experience with his own guns under differing conditions. For shore bombardment onto these, of course, are added the adjustments for range and bearing offsets and for target elevation. By "added" is meant the net sum of all the pluses and minuses, both in range and right and left in deflection.

Now, after the foregoing, one can understand what a great achievement it is when a ship's battery straddles with

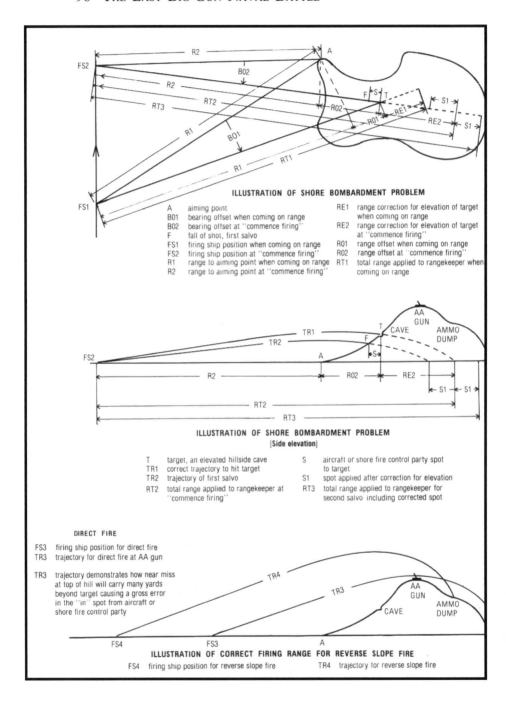

ILLUSTRATION OF SHORE BOMBARDMENT PROBLEM

A	aiming point	RE1	range correction for elevation of target when coming on range
B02	bearing offset when coming on range	RE2	range correction for elevation of target at "commence firing"
B02	bearing offset at "commence firing"		
F	fall of shot, first salvo	R01	range offset when coming on range
FS1	firing ship position when coming on range	R02	range offset at "commence firing"
FS2	firing ship position at "commence firing"	RT1	total range applied to rangekeeper when coming on range
R1	range to aiming point when coming on range		
R2	range to aiming point at "commence firing"		

ILLUSTRATION OF SHORE BOMBARDMENT PROBLEM
[Side elevation]

T	target, an elevated hillside cave	S	aircraft or shore fire control party spot to target
TR1	correct trajectory to hit target		
TR2	trajectory of first salvo	S1	spot applied after correction for elevation
RT2	total range applied to rangekeeper at "commence firing"	RT3	total range applied to rangekeeper for second salvo including corrected spot

DIRECT FIRE

FS3 firing ship position for direct fire
TR3 trajectory for direct fire at AA gun

TR3 trajectory demonstrates how near miss at top of hill will carry many yards beyond target causing a gross error in the "in" spot from aircraft or shore fire control party

ILLUSTRATION OF CORRECT FIRING RANGE FOR REVERSE SLOPE FIRE

FS4 firing ship position for reverse slope fire   TR4 trajectory for reverse slope fire the first salvo. Later, it will be seen how remarkable, should an early hit be obtained.

In shore bombardment there are additional complications, displayed in the bottom diagram. If we happen to be direct firing at a hilltop gun emplacement, and we miss just a bit over, the salvo may travel hundreds of yards down the backslope. An "in spot" from our observation plane, or from the shore fire control party, could be grossly inaccurate. If such a spot should be applied without thought, the resultant salvo may land among our own troops.

Another difficult feat is reverse slope fire at a target situated like the ammunition dump shown. In this case, the firing vessel must move out to sea to enable the shells to clear the crest. This sometimes requires much communication and explanation between the firing ship and the flagship. There may be someone who thinks we are retreating!

Also, if our observation pilot is circling and under fire, he may become impatient at the delay.

9

THE LAST BIG-GUN NAVAL BATTLE

The next assault was debated at the highest levels: Should we or should we not bypass the Philippines and land on Formosa [Taiwan]? There were strong strategic reasons for advancing the Pacific campaign to Formosa, closer to the Japanese mainland. But General MacArthur forcefully argued that the U.S. had a moral obligation to the Philippines. For four years the Filipinos had mounted a fierce resistance to the Japanese, relying on MacArthur's promise to return. Leyte Gulf in the Philippines was finally selected as the most suitable landing area.

The gunfire support group for the operation in the Philippines included many cruisers, several destroyer divisions, and six old battleships, *West Virginia, Maryland, California, Tennessee, Pennsylvania* and *Mississippi*. The first five battleships were Pearl Harbor veterans. *West Virginia* was on her first operation after repair and modernization. Vice Admiral Jesse B. Oldendorf, USN, in USS *Louisville* (CA-28), commanded the group, and Rear Admiral Ruddock, in *West Virginia*, was COMBATDIV 4.

With the arrival of so many fast, new 16-inch-gunned ships, we began to doubt that *Maryland* would participate in a major battleship battle. Nevertheless, the main and secondary battery fire control parties continued

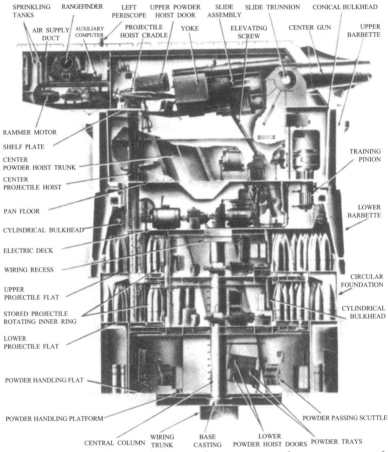

Cutaway view of 16-inch turret showing general arrangement of equipment. U.S. Navy

drilling for surface action, and we still carried the armor-piercing shells for the big guns and what were called "common" shells for the secondary. The common shells were especially designed for use against such thin-skinned vessels as destroyers and submarines. They would penetrate, but not too much. The armor-piercing shells had been known to pass completely through an unprotected target ship, creating consternation and fine stories, but relatively small damage.

Wall of the barbette of USS New Jersey *(BB-62) lined with 16-inch shells. Civilian visitor shows comparative size of shells. George F. Gruner.*

The turret crews had fired so much in bombardment, it was almost routine. For surface action the crews merely had to substitute the armor-piercing for the high-capacity shells and use full-service propelling charges rather than the reduced bombardment loads.

Secured below each turret and standing chest high, the 16-inch armor-piercing projectiles were an impressive sight. Each weighed 2,240 pounds, but, surprisingly, contained only 35 pounds of explosive. That was sufficient when it detonated after penetration in a confined space, as we discovered in the Roi Island blockhouse "Bruce." The service propelling charge consisted of five 125 pound powder bags, each with the black powder ignition charge attached to its base.

The propelling charge itself is worthy of note in that it was not just a bag of random small granules as might be imagined. Instead, each particle was a carefully

Magazine of USS New Jersey *(BB-62) with powder bags stowed in canisters. Note loading tray in foreground. Crewman unidentified. George F. Gruner.*

designed small cylinder with several holes running longitudinally. The purpose was to produce a controlled burn in the gunpowder chamber. This resulted in a powerful but steady push up the bore, rather than a violent, uncontrolled explosion.

Our 16-inch 45-caliber main battery guns had the same basic design as the 5-inch 51-caliber secondary battery guns. The interior of the breeches had interrupted screw threads. The breech plugs had matching threads which mated with the breech threads when the plugs were inserted and rotated. In both guns the plugs carried a mushroom-shaped steel piece. When the guns fired, gas pressure forced the mushroom aft against a seal. This seal compressed and expanded in diameter to prevent the gases from escaping.

In both guns hot gases and burning embers remaining in the powder chambers from a previous round were expelled by the high pressure gas ejection compressed air. This air was automatically injected when the breech plugs were opened. A difficulty with both guns was that even with the gas ejection air, a burning ember could adhere to the mushroom face. This, of course, could be disastrous should that ember contact the black powder at the base of the next round's after propelling powder bag before the breech was fully closed.

Both guns were fired by a combination percussion and electric primer, which was inserted into the firing lock prior to each round. This lock was mounted at the center of the after side of the plug. Both guns also had a salvo latch, the function of which will be explained later.

Interior turret area of the USS New Jersey *(BB-62). Note open breech plug (gun elevated) and recoil cylinders. George F. Gruner.*

Our 16-inch main battery guns and our 5-inch secondary guns differed in two important ways:

The 5-inch breech plug opened and then swung to the side. The plugman could easily insert the next primer. The 16-inch plug opened and then swung down. The plugman could not reach the firing lock with a primer.

Second, our 5-inch guns could be loaded at any angle of elevation. Because of the weight and size of its ammunition, the 16-inch had to be returned to a loading position with just a slight elevation after each round was fired. [See Appendix A for complete description of loading procedures in a 16-inch turret.]

As we advanced across the Pacific toward Leyte the invasion force grew in size and power. Admiral Kinkaid's Seventh Fleet, under General MacArthur's command, numbered 738 ships, and Admiral Halsey's Third Fleet, under the direction of Admiral Nimitz, included seventeen fast carriers, six new battleships, seventeen cruisers, and fifty-eight destroyers. For local air support eighteen escort carriers in three task units were assigned to the Seventh Fleet.

The task facing Admiral Halsey was formidable. The Philippine Islands and Formosa with their land-based air could be considered unsinkable aircraft carriers around which the Japanese Fleet might still operate. Just before and during the operation, Admiral Halsey's Third Fleet neutralized many of those island air strips and reduced the number of enemy aircraft which could be staged to attack.

Minesweepers swept ahead as we prepared to enter Leyte Gulf, but from our foretop vantage point we observed the crews of Turrets I and II as they launched our paravanes[1] for the first time in a combat area.

---

[1] Paravanes resemble torpedoes, but have a stabilizer and no rudder. Two stubby wings extend from the sides, and there is a wire-cutting device at the forward end. This equipment is the warships' defense against the anchored mine.

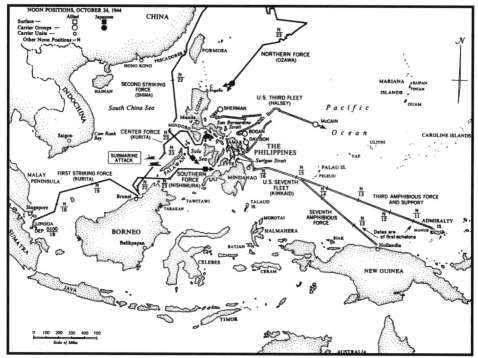

Approach of the fleets to Leyte Gulf. World War II.

As our column advanced into Leyte Gulf, all hands topside kept a careful watch for mines which might pop up aft of our paravanes, or from the paravanes of the ships ahead. We didn't surface any, but *California* did. Rifle fire from the "Prune Barge" drew our attention to a round black mine with those ominous horns rolling in the small chop. It was harmlessly exploded, and we saw no more, but the paravanes in the six big ships were not streamed in vain.

Bombardment of Red and White Beaches on Leyte Island commenced well in advance and continued right up until the massive landings at 1000, October 20, 1944. We fired the usual area coverages, and we again fired missions with our own aircraft as spotters.

There was a near tragedy when one of our OS2Us collided with one from *Mississippi*. Our aircraft returned with the other plane's wing pontoon embedded in its right wing.

Due to our previous experience, our bombardment mission seemed almost routine, but there is another aspect of the operation to which most naval histories give less than adequate attention. Our navigators faced a special problem in Leyte Gulf. We had charts for the area, but they were uncorrected. Water depths change; there may be new obstructions such as sunken ships, uncharted coral heads and so forth. *Maryland* drew an average of thirty-four feet. There were many spots in Leyte Gulf we couldn't go. That wasn't the problem. What taxed our navigator's skills were the locations where we *might* be able to go and where the gunnery officer wished to go to execute a certain important fire-support mission. The chart showed sufficient water to satisfy the unseasoned, but not enough extra to make the navigator completely comfortable.

There was one occasion where we came close to grounding, but backed away in time. It's awful to see that muddy water coming up alongside.

West Virginia did touch one of her screws on an obstruction and had to steam all the way back to Espiritu Santo for repair.

Many navigators, when they hear of a grounding, exclaim, "There, but for the grace of God, go I." It's an overused phrase, perhaps, but in the navigator's case, this is a kind of fervent prayer for business-like, reliable, seven-day-a-week divine intervention.

The decisive Battle for Leyte Gulf was four separate actions: Sibuyan Sea, Surigao, Samar and Cape Engano, October 23-26, 1944. Taken as a whole, it was the greatest naval battle in history. Two hundred eighty-two ships engaged, with over 185,000 officers and men, resulting in the destruction of the Japanese Fleet as an effective fighting force. The Battle of Surigao Strait (October 24-25) is considered the U.S. Navy's greatest single triumph; the night action, in particular, a model of timing, coordination and almost perfect execution.

Afternoon, October 24, 1944.   We were in our foretop general quarters stations when about twenty motor torpedo boats raced by.

We always enjoyed watching from the foretop the action on the flag and navigating bridges far below. This time, there was a lot of dispatch reading and spirited conversation. Much to the director crews' amusement, I focused my 7 x 50 glass and tried to read the dispatches. I could make out a few words, but the officers would not hold still long enough to make out the entire message.

The battleships and cruisers launched all their observation planes. As the sun slipped below the Leyte hills, we formed up and steamed south.

There was no official word, but we began to understand: the torpedo boats were speeding toward Surigao Strait and we were following.

Dimly seen in the twilight were the older capital ships of the Battle Line of the United States:

West Virginia 16-inch, eight guns.
Maryland   16-inch, eight guns.
Mississippi   14-inch, twelve guns.
Tennessee   14-inch, twelve guns.
California   14-inch, twelve guns.
Pennsylvania 14-inch, twelve guns.

The battle line, under orders from Admiral Oldendorf, took position where we could steam slowly east and west, blocking the south entrance to Leyte Gulf from Surigao Strait.

The eight cruisers were divided into two groups and moved to both flanks. The eastern ships were

The Japanese battleship Yamato *carried 18.1-inch guns and displaced 63,000 tons. Author.*

Louisville, Portland, Minneapolis, Denver, and *Columbia.* To the west waited *Shropshire, Boise,* and *Phoenix.*

Destroyers patrolled below the cruisers, and thirty-nine torpedo boats were stationed down the Strait and in the Mindanao Sea. Their function was to attack with torpedoes and, even more important, to serve as scouts and report the enemy's movements to the admiral.

To the north, the mass of vulnerable invasion, supply and service vessels, which we were protecting, slowly disappeared in the gathering gloom, There were bursts of tracers from an occasional or suspected air raid. The entire force was on edge that night.

How fared the people? You might say surface action was our bread and butter. We were raised and trained in its traditions. We were at home with our functions. Intense interest and increasingly fierce but well-controlled excitement seemed to be the prevalent mood over the telephones and throughout the ship as we awaited the oncoming enemy.

Although we had them out-gunned and out-numbered, we felt some fear. HMS *Hood* and HMS *Prince of Wales* versus *Bismarck* in the North Atlantic in 1941 loomed in our subconscious. They were three bustling, sea-going small cities, full of life, activity and fun, like ours. *Bismarck* was outnumbered, but *Hood* and her crew went — except three men — in a blinding flash.

Hyuga, *right, and* Ise, below, *were combined battleship/aircraft carriers. Left, U.S. Navy, below,* Battleships and Battle- cruisers.

Our ships were in position — *Maryland* steaming after *West Virginia*, followed by *Mississippi* and the others. Our skipper, Captain Ray, who had served in the Philippines at the beginning of the war, came on the loud- speaker system and gave all hands the latest information:

Japanese battleship Fuso *in drydock at Kure, Japan.* Battleships and Battlecruisers.

Battleship Yamashiro *undergoing trials in 1934. Note "pagoda" style superstructure developed by Japan between World Wars.* Battleships and Battlecruisers.

The Japanese warships were out, all of them. The enemy fleet was divided into three groups, perhaps four.

First, a center force of battleships and others (18.1-inch *Yamato*, 18.1-inch *Musashi*, 16-inch *Nagato*, 14-inch *Kongo*, 14-inch *Haruna*, nine cruisers and thirteen destroyers) was heading for San Bernardino Strait, just north of Samar Island. It sustained submarine attack, and heavy attack by Admiral Halsey's Third Fleet aircraft.

Second, there was an enemy decoy northern force with aircraft carriers (four carriers, two converted battleship-carriers — 14-inch *Hyuga* and 14-inch *Ise* —three light cruisers, and eight destroyers). Admiral Halsey was steaming north after them.

Captain Ray concluded with reports of one or two groups, including battleships, which were driving through the Mindanao Sea toward Surigao Strait.[2]

It was electrifying news. The old, slow battleships, five the victims of the Pearl Harbor attack, replaced by the new, fast battleships and displaced by the carriers would have their chance. Revenge was at hand. We would be participating in what could be one of the great battles of World War II.

---

[2] There were two groups: the first group had 14-inch *Yamashiro*, 14-inch *Fuso*, heavy cruiser *Mogami*, and four destroyers, and the second group was composed of heavy cruisers *Nachi* and *Ashigara*, light cruiser *Abukuma* and four destroyers.

We quietly went to our battle stations from which we had secured for a "battle dinner;" then did a painstakingly careful check of all systems, set the watertight doors and hatches. "All stations manned . . ."

Throughout the battle line, preparations continued. Perhaps the busiest were the men on the shell decks below the turret gunrooms. They were setting aside the high capacity bombardment shells and loading the shell hoists with tough, steel-nosed armor-piercing projectiles. In the powder magazines other men made ready the full-service powder charges; chief warrant gunners traversed the magazine areas, taking room temperatures, checking the ammunition and the ammunition handlers, adjusting ammunition supply plans to the anticipated needs of the forthcoming engagement.

The navigators and their assistants studied the charts of the probable battle area, spotting reefs and other dangers to navigation, checking tide levels and currents; visibility, wind, and sea conditions.

In the plotting rooms below the armored decks the main battery fire control officers and their assistants calculated their initial ballistics, as did those in the secondary plotting rooms of the modernized ships — *West Virginia, California,* and *Tennessee.*

Combat information center personnel had all their equipment in operation, prepared to pick up, track, evaluate, and report all incoming surface and air contacts, and process submarine reports from the destroyers and search aircraft.

The damage controlmen laid out firefighting and damage-repair equipment while damage control officers reviewed the status of the fuel and water tanks for possible counterflooding to quickly remove any list resulting from underwater damage. They knew that extreme lists to the firing side would reduce the maximum ranges of the main and secondary batteries.

USS Pennsylvania *leading the pre-war American battle line, much as it appeared at the Battle of Surigao Strait.* Battleships and Battlecruisers.

The doctors and hospital corpsmen prepared the operating rooms for casualties and, on our ship, the junior officers' wardroom was set up as a standby operating room in case sick bay should be hit.

The engineering department had all eight boilers on the line, prepared for maximum speed, emergency maneuvers, and possible damage to any unit of their huge plant — the firerooms, two turboelectric alternators, four propulsion motors, shafts, bearings, screws, condensers, switchboards, pumps . . .

The radiomen received all encrypted traffic and decoded it. All the communicators were standing by for possible emergency messages "in the clear" — uncoded.

No signal flags at night, of course, but the crew on *Maryland*'s signal bridge was on the alert for possible sightings of signal, identification, or emergency riding lights.

The supply departments were cleaning up after the battle dinners — 2,162 of them. With everything ready, all hands settled down. The machinery quietly hummed, the radarmen concentrated on their scopes, the lookouts endlessly scanned the black horizon. The helmsmen steered their courses and stood waiting at their tillers for sudden orders. For such great ships steered by huge rudders, the helms were ridiculously small six-inch brass bars with a handle. They resembled the controls motormen use on street cars.

The chaplains, often the best-liked officers aboard, were everywhere. Their mere appearance reassured us. Their presence reminded one of home, choirs singing, church doors open . . .

Our captain sat in his chair or roved his bridge, acknowledging all the reports received.

The Japanese plan was to have the center force hit the front gate. While we were engaging this stronger fleet, the southern foxes would run up the back and catch our defenseless hindquarter. Their northern ships would entice our Third Fleet away into another area.

Admiral Halsey unwittingly took the bait. His Third Fleet ran north to take on Matsuda's decoy fleet. In so doing Halsey missed the opportunity to demolish the center force, either by aircraft attack, or by gunfire, should it still manage to sortie from San Bernardino Strait.

We talked in the quiet foretop as *Maryland* crept back and forth across the Strait. We didn't know too much, but, like all sailors, we could speculate.

Squalls were reported in the area, but for us it was an increasingly overcast, black night, strangely still. The sea was smooth, the visibility good. Since we had no secondary battery radar, we practiced more than most on the development of night vision. You don't look directly at the object you wish to see. Using that technique, we could make out the looming darker shapes of the nearby vessels.

We knew the pressure on us would be strong to take under fire any closing shadow, but we knew the Japanese cruisers and destroyers were capable of launching their torpedoes at great distances and probably would — well beyond our visual range.

If we opened with our main battery at, say, 20,000 yards, the enemy would probably send their torpedoes, using our gun flashes as aiming points.

We did not do column movements at each side of the Strait, but executed simultaneous 180-degree ship turns. This put *West Virginia* in the van heading east, and it made *Pennsylvania* the lead ship heading west. It was similar to the maneuver used at Jutland by German Admiral Scheer, except the Germans turned away from the Grand Fleet by a "ripple" movement starting from the rear.

Our orders to turn were sent over the TBS radio (Talk Between Ships) by direction of the admiral as:

"'Bulldogs, turn 18." (All battleships turn right 180 degrees in unison.)

"Bulldogs, stand by, turn 18."

"Bulldogs, execute, turn 18." (All rudders went over to the right the "standard" amount, which was the proper rudder angle to complete a turn with the pre-designated diameter.)[3]

To turn left the signal would be "18 turn."

We had practiced that maneuver and now came out right in line, the same distance apart but heading in the opposite direction.

---

[3] Every class and type of ship had a different standard rudder angle. It was usually determined by experimentation during fleet exercises. Author's note: I *think* ours was seventeen-and-a-half degrees, but that was fifty-five years ago.

We began to see light flashes to the south — the loom of searchlights the enemy used to illuminate our attacking PTs. The Japanese had arrived.

0230, October 25, 1944: Destroyer Squadron 54, five ships commanded by Captain Jesse B. Coward, USN, began its torpedo attacks down both sides of the Strait. About ten minutes later, Destroyer Squadron 24, with Captain K. M. McManes, USN, commanding, attacked down the west side.

Aboard *West Virginia* Admiral Ruddock was on the flag bridge. Captain H. V. Wiley, USN, was her commanding officer; Lieutenant Commander Thomas Lombardi, USNR was spot 1; Lieutenant Robert Baumrucker, USNR, was spot 2 in the maintop; and Lieutenant Edward J. Fruechtl, USN, was main battery plotting room officer.

Early on, *West Virginia*'s director developed a malfunction which took its Mark 8 radar out of action. Control was shifted to the maintop where Baumrucker's Mark 8 picked up the enemy at 44,000 yards. Time, 0304. At 42,000 yards the radar screen showed two large objects.

Battleship *Fuso* received torpedoes from our destroyers at 0309. She exploded. She broke in two. She burned, both bow and stern sinking later. Battleship *Yamashiro* was hit by one or two torpedoes between 0325 and 0340. The damage was aft in the port rudder area. She continued her attack with little speed reduction. Destroyers *Yamagumo* and *Michishio* were torpedoed and sunk, and a third destroyer, *Asagumo*, severely damaged by those classic destroyer torpedo attacks, the dream of every "tin can" sailor.

Asagumo was later sunk by our cruisers and destroyers.

0351: the first cruisers, *Louisville* on our left flank and *Boise* on our right flank, commenced firing.

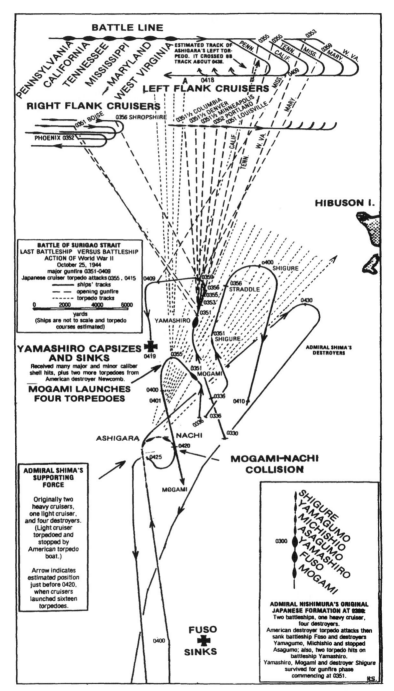

Battle of Surigao Strait. U.S. Naval Historical Center.

Suddenly, there was a great deal to see as all the cruisers joined from both sides of the channel. The 6-inch light cruisers fired so rapidly each kept four or five salvos in the air following one another in their beautifully curved trajectories. The 8-inch heavy cruisers' fire was more deliberate, but their salvo intervals were amazingly brief.

Hundreds of red tracers were converging on, or near, one spot. Through our binoculars and director scopes we caught sight of a Japanese battleship (*Yamashiro*, we later learned) with its high, pagoda-type mast. The frequent topside hits lighted that ship and the forest of surrounding shell splashes.

"Range, 24,000 yards, closing," from the ship's gunnery circuit talker. Our main battery was trained to starboard, the guns were elevated as we steamed on.

Looking down the Strait, we saw tracers emerging from that central point. The Japanese were returning the fire. But *Maryland* had no targets on her fire-control radar.

0352:10: the range was decreasing. Then, out of the dark just ahead, *West Virginia* ("Weevie") fired her first salvo, range 22,400 yards. Her tracers raced away. Fire to starboard, abaft the beam. Thirty-five seconds later off went another from "Weevie" — up and away went the tracers.

Captain Wiley, Lieutenant Baumrucker, and others, saw explosions on their target's forecastle and foremast structure when their first salvos hit. Had *Yamashiro* been so obliging as to sink right then, *West Virginia* would have a claim to all-time naval top gun honors.

Aboard *Maryland*, at one instant during the action, I did see an especially brilliant flash, which could have been an exploding ship.

Our ships were all in range of the Japanese "Long Lance" torpedoes, but they scored no hits. This fine result

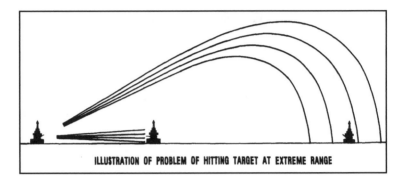

ILLUSTRATION OF PROBLEM OF HITTING TARGET AT EXTREME RANGE

could have been due, partly at least, to the turns made by our battleships and cruisers after the beginning of our gunfire.

Still, *Maryland*'s guns were silent.

"Shoot! Shoot! Shoot!" the men on our two directors were pleading.

We *had* to participate after the long years of practicing and waiting. Horrible to come all that way, and not get in a single shot. We anxiously watched the battle in the distance.

West Virginia, Tennessee, and *California,* the recently modernized ships, had Mark 8, Mod. 2 main battery fire control radars, which were superior to the Mark 3s carried by *Maryland, Mississippi,* and *Pennsylvania.*

The OTC, [Officer in Tactical Command] Rear Admiral G. L. Weyler, USN, then made an excellent move:

"All bulldogs, turn 3; all bulldogs, turn 3." (All battleships turn together thirty degrees to the right.)

"All bulldogs, turn 3, stand by."

"All bulldogs, execute turn 3. I repeat; all bulldogs, execute turn 3."

0355: as can be seen on the chart, this turn in unison closed the range, brought the targets forward of the starboard beam, but still kept the ships from interfering with each others' lines of sight. To conceive and successfully execute such a maneuver with six monstrous ships traveling at night during the battle's fury was an awesome accomplishment.

The tension and frustration were agonizing. The minutes ticked on.

"Shoot, shoot, *please* shoot!"

West Virginia, Tennessee and *California* were firing at a great rate. *Maryland, Mississippi*, and *Pennsylvania* were painfully silent.

Lieutenant James A. Dare, USN — later, admiral, and he earned it — still our spot 1 officer in the foretop just over our heads, was up to the challenge.

"We came to shoot. We *will* shoot," he said, but still no ship signal on his radar. There were signals reflected from *West Virginia*'s massive splashes around the target.

Lt. Dare took off a series of ranges and bearings on those splashes and sent them down to plot. There, Mr. Lowerre and his people roughly averaged them into the rangekeeper for an adequate firing setup.

Main battery warning buzzer: "Buzzzzz, buzzzzzzz."

We closed our eyes and held our earphones against our ears. We had never experienced an eight-gun service salvo at that high angle before, but we wanted it to go. Gosh, we sure wanted it to go!

But — silence.

Maryland's big guns sat there, trained forward of the beam, due to the turn. Then, finally, "Buzz, buzz, buzzzzzzzz — KLAMMO!"

0359:

Off they went — all eight guns — adding our projectile weight to that of *West Virginia* and the other firing ships. Finally, finally, finally *Maryland* was doing what she was designed and built to do, what her crew was recruited and trained to do, what we had practiced so many hundreds of hours to do.

Up and up climbed the eight tracers; down, down, they went into that maelstrom of flashes and splashes miles away.

We rode the mast as it lashed to and fro, as a tree moves in a strong gale. We forgot about the flash and shock, as everyone strained to see how our tracers were doing, We wanted *Maryland* to get some hits!

How could we be sure of an armor-piercing shell hit at night at that range? It would have to cause a huge explosion.

The people on the guns and in the magazines wanted to know what was happening. The port side gun crews couldn't see a thing. We saw everything from secondary forward and tried to keep the gun captains informed so they could tell the crews, who phoned down to the magazines.

Maryland's tracers disappeared into that converging point down the Strait. Four battleships were now firing in addition to the smaller ships. It was impossible to tell which was which in that great semicircle of fire, with the storm of tracers concentrating on nearly a single spot . . .

Crossing the 'T': A classic naval maneuver between men-o'-war. Japanese Admiral Togo did it to the Russians just after the turn of the twentieth century in the battle of Tsushima. British Admiral Jellicoe did it to the Germans in World War I. The ships on the cross bar of the T fire full broadsides. Only the ships at the top of the stem can return fire with their bow guns while those behind lose their lines of sight in the gunsmoke. This was what Admiral Oldendorf had prepared for the Japanese southern forces. Because the Japanese had been in the naval business for centuries and Togo was their hero, one can't help wondering how could they have allowed themselves to get into such a predicament.

Heavy cruiser *Mogami* and destroyer *Shigure* were still with *Yamashiro* at 0351 when our fleet opened the gunfire phase. *Yamashiro* was hit repeatedly, and erupted in flame. Both her main and secondary batteries were in action, and she made hits on destroyer USS *Albert W. Grant* (DD-649). *Yamashiro* turned left about 100 degrees at 0359, and again left 90 degrees at 0409 while still under heavy gunfire. At about 0411 two more torpedoes slammed into her starboard quarter. These were delivered by a destroyer, USS *Newcomb* (DL-586), one of the nine-ship Squadron 56, commanded by Captain Roland Smoot, USN.

Mogami was hit by two shells shortly after 0351, which started a fire. At 0355, with a range of about 25,000 yards to the American battle line and 17,000 yards to our western cruisers, she launched four torpedoes aimed at gun flashes to her north.

Mogami then turned south and soon received three more direct shell hits, two of which detonated on the bridge. All there were killed, including the commanding officer, the navigator, the communications officer, the torpedo officer, and, reportedly, the executive officer. Under the gunnery officer's command, she continued south while her people fought the fires. There were twelve torpedoes remaining and the crew succeeded in jettisoning five. The last seven were exploded by the fire, but, surprisingly, this dampened the flames and eased the firefighters' work. A tough ship. (She had also undergone severe damage during the later stages of the Battle of Midway.)

Shigure, a destroyer famous in the Japanese Navy for her prior combat achievements, was destined to be the lone survivor of Admiral Nishimura's force. She made the closest approach to our major units: about 15,000 yards to us, and our left flank cruisers were only about 11,000 yards away. *Shigure*, however, did not fire her torpedoes from this favorable attack position. She suffered one hit, which did not explode, and also damage from many near misses.

Maryland fired six eight-gun salvos and our battle line executed another simultaneous turn — to course west — during the tumult of gunfire.

We were then firing to port, my side, but soon, at about 0409, we were forced to cease fire as the damaged destroyer, *Albert W. Grant*, was unable to clear the target area. She had received attention from the gunners on both sides for a total of nineteen hits.

Mississippi fired one salvo aimed at *Yamashiro* at 0409. *Pennsylvania*, her range fouled by our attacking destroyers, was unable to open. On board battered *Yamashiro* the crew was ordered to abandon ship. At 0419, just two minutes later, she capsized and sank.

At this juncture, Admiral Shima arrived in the battle area on board heavy cruiser *Nachi*, followed by heavy cruiser *Ashigara* and four destroyers. *Nachi* had passed the floating sections of *Fuso* about 0400, and it had been assumed for some time these were the hulks of both *Yamashiro* and *Fuso*. This distressing presumption could have influenced later combat decisions. The admiral's confidence was probably already shaken by light cruiser *Abukuma*'s departure from his line. She took a torpedo in her vitals from torpedo boat *PT-137*, commanded by Lieutenant (jg) Isadore M. Kovar, USNR.

Soon after passing *Fuso*'s remains, Admiral Shima and his staff probably sighted the cruelly hit and flaming *Mogami* on their starboard bow, range roughly 12,000 yards. Beyond her, but fine on the bow to starboard, the burning and exploding *Yamashiro* had to be coming into view unless obscured by the heavy smoke.

The admiral released his destroyers, *Shiranuhi, Kasumi, Ushio* and *Akebono*, for torpedo attacks, swung into a column turn to his right, and, just before 0420, on the basis of a possible radar contact, allowed a total of sixteen torpedoes to be launched by the two cruisers. These weapons were reported to have been set to run in a spread centered on a base course of 025 degrees true, to the east of the central position of our battle line, then heading west. The range to us, by rough estimate, was 29,000 yards. By then, *Yamashiro*, on fire, dead in the water, and sinking, was only a few miles almost directly north of *Nachi*. As *Nachi* continued her turn to her right, the relative bearing of *Mogami*, close aboard, was moving down *Nachi*'s port side. This could give the illusion on board *Nachi* that *Mogami* was dead in the water. She was not. (See chart). She was moving south at about 8 knots under crude steering control from steering aft.

Nachi was struck on her port quarter by the almost unmaneuverable *Mogami*, damaging that beleaguered vessel even more and partially flooding *Nachi*'s steering aft. Slowed to 18 knots, having almost completed a circle, *Nachi* and *Ashigara* were again heading north into battle.

Admiral Shima, however, evidently having decided the possible gains were not worth the obvious risks, ordered a temporary retirement. His plan was to regroup the surviving ships and then make a more organized attack.

Nachi then turned left and led *Ashigara*, the destroyers, and, for awhile, *Mogami*, to the south.

None of Admiral Shima's destroyers was able to complete a torpedo attack, probably because there were no longer any gun flashes from our now silent task group to serve as aiming points. They did, according to Japanese records, make a run to a good position in the northeast, and, turning, had to increase speed to overhaul the cruisers. *Albert W. Grant*'s tragic predicament, which halted our gunfire at 0409, produced an important benefit for them.

Destroyer *Shiranuhi* and the torpedoed light cruiser *Abukuma* later were sunk by our aircraft. The remainder of Admiral Shima's force survived.

The *Mogami*, lagging behind, was taken under fire at 0525 by our pursuing cruisers. She then underwent air attack at 0902. That started a major fire, which finally forced the crew to abandon. Destroyer *Akebono* was ordered to dispatch this warship with torpedoes, and she went under at 1307.

At Surigao, the Allies overwhelming power, utilized effectively, resulted in major victory at small cost.

10

AFTERMATH

At daybreak we could see none of the Japanese ships. The two battleships and the two destroyers had sunk. Over the horizon, badly damaged *Asagumo* awaited her fate. The cruisers and the remaining destroyers were driven back. The sole occupant of the oil-covered waters was *Albert W. Grant*.

But there was more work to do. Admiral Oldendorf with a few of his cruisers and destroyers took up pursuit of the survivors to the south, while we with our escorts hastened northeast in the gathering light to form another battle line, this time across the east entrance to Leyte Gulf.

Admiral Kurita was knocking at our little escort carriers outside with his mighty 18.1-inch *Yamato* and her accomplices, the 16-inch *Nagato*, 14-inch *Kongo*, 14-inch *Haruna*, the heavy and light cruisers, and the destroyers of

Haruna as she appeared in 1934 undergoing trials after reconstruction. Imperial War Museum.

his center force. The membership of his gun club had been depleted during the days before by the loss of 18.1-inch *Musashi* and several cruisers to our submarine and air attacks. They sortied from San Bernardino Strait to the north at 0035 this same morning and steamed down to enter Leyte Gulf from the east to attack the transports landing our invasion fleet.

If they had not been rebuffed by Admiral Kincaid's escort carriers, what a rumble their arrival would have stirred up among the gallant old fossils with the smoking guns just completing that little dust-up at Surigao!

It is history that the Japanese center force did not attempt to enter Leyte Gulf, but turned back after engaging one of our escort carrier task groups outside. The Battle of Surigao Strait was the last big-gun naval battle — the last old-line battleship vs. battleship combat — and doubtless the last Crossing of the 'T'.

The Japanese lost thousands of men in the two battleships, two cruisers and three destroyers sunk. We suffered 39 Americans killed and 114 wounded. We lost one PT boat.

Yamashiro, Fuso and the Japanese destroyers rest there as memorials to those thousands of men who obeyed orders and did their best. The valiant *Mogami* and cruiser *Abukuma* have their special places to the south. The ships of the old U.S. battle line are gone.

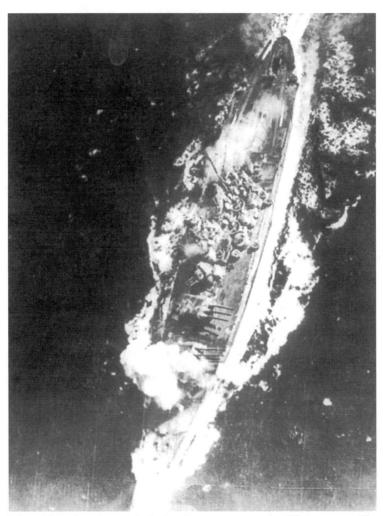

Musashi *under air attack during her run across the Sibuyan sea. She was sunk by aircraft before engaging any U.S. warships. Imperial War Museum.*

Now, all the great guns of Surigao Strait are silent forever.

11

KAMIKAZE!

November 25, 1944. Now, we were in the endgame. After the disastrous defeat of the Japanese southern force, the ferocity of their air attacks increased. The first was a formal daylight dive-bomb attack by a complete squadron. They came in fairly high, but easily visible. Our escort carrier air groups, which normally supplied the combat air patrol, were away, engaged in attacks on Admiral Kurita's fleet outside Leyte Gulf.

The Japanese came in perfect formation, six groups of three aircraft each, on a course directly toward our battle line. Then, to our astonishment, they peeled off one by one into dives on a screening destroyer ahead and slightly to starboard.

With six big, slow battleships in sight, ready to engage their center force battle line, they released their bombs at the destroyer, pulled out, and were gone.

All eighteen aircraft missed their target.

It was like no other attack we ever observed. The destroyer fired with all batteries, but she made no dramatic maneuvers. That the entire Japanese squadron was incompetent was unthinkable, yet — what other explanation could there be?

Earlier, we witnessed another unusual aircraft torpedo attack. On October 20, at Leyte Gulf, after we had secured from general quarters, a single enemy aircraft suddenly came in over the hills.

The starboard 5-inch antiaircraft control officer had just climbed out of his Mark 19 director, and I was about to take over as his condition watch relief. We kept the 5-inch antiaircraft battery at least partially manned twenty-four hours a day. This was called the "condition watch" and it required help from the officers and men of the secondary battery.

That torpedo plane dived to the surface and flew through the entire fleet without a shot being fired. It delivered its torpedo into a cruiser's side (USS *Honolulu* CL-48 which survived but spent the rest of the war under repair from the effects of the torpedo) and sped away — home in time for dinner!

That day in Leyte Gulf, the condition watch had been set, rangekeeper and director power was off, half the guns were secured, and the ready ammunition boxes were closed. The crews, although not asleep, were at ease.

The cruiser USS Honolulu *(CL-48). U.S. Naval Photographic Center.*

The moment I spotted the torpedo plane, I headed for the director, but stopped as I saw it was too late. We were in the center of a mass of ships, the target passing behind one ship after another, and it was past our starboard beam and drawing away. The target cruiser was well to the south, and she was presenting her port side to the attacker.

To fire the battery, I would have had to wiggle into the control officer's seat, thrust my head through the topside hatch, don the headphones, and call: "Torpedo plane attack, starboard; all guns match your pointers — stand by!"

The gun crew would have had to take their stations, open the ready boxes, and pass the shells with the attached powder cases to the mounts. The fusesetter would match his pointers as the new signals came down from the director. This would keep the fuses of the three shells resting in the fuse pots correctly set for the projected time of flight. That, of course, would not apply to any proximity fuses used. When each trainer matched his pointers, he would have to swing his mount from the search sector to the firing position. (The gun captain usually pushed on the gun shield to help the mount swing faster. You could do this on the 5-inch, 25-caliber, but not on the heavier, twin mount 5-inch 38's many of the new ships carried. The latter had power, but it takes time to start the motors and cut them in.) The pointers, meanwhile, would have matched their pointers, closed and locked their firing keys.

From me to the director pointer and trainer: "Torpedo plane, bearing zero seven zero, moving left, elevation two degrees. There he is! He just came out from behind that big transport!" To the rangekeeper and rangefinder operators, "Target angle, two five zero, speed one two zero, range three five double oh!"

The rangekeeper operator would crank in that info, and, after the director pointer and trainer had settled on the target, the rangefinder operator would send (electrically) the rangekeeper an accurate series of ranges. Tracking, the rangekeeper operator would quickly have a solution. He would have tapped my foot, "Set up!"

"Commence firing, commence firing!"

Each gun captain would yell something like, "Go!" The loaders would grab the first shells from the fuse pots and slam them into the loading trays. Their rammermen would smash them home.

"Crack, crack, crack . . ." the wild, mean, ear-shattering voice of the antiaircraft batteries.

We could all have worked fast, faster than anyone may imagine, but it would take seconds — say, thirty seconds — if there were no glitches. After thirty seconds, the target would have been about 2,000 yards farther away. It would have doubled its closest range in only a minute.

If I had been in the director seat where I belonged, instead of standing outside in sky control, talking to the officer I was relieving, *Maryland* might have gotten off at least a warning shot or two. It would have alerted the cruiser gun crews, and they may have been able to fire their automatic weapons.

Dozens of ships, hundreds of guns, broad daylight, yet not a single shot fired. I have no explanation.

The Japanese, surprisingly and fortunately, did not try too many of those low-level, single plane, conventional sneak attacks. It may be wondered, after that rousing success against our antiaircraft defenses, why not?

That was one of the last conventional attacks *Maryland* encountered.

Suddenly, we were provided front row seats from which we could observe one of the great tragic dramas of history. The effect on us would remain for all our lives. Even now, writing this, my ears ring, my heart beats faster, the adrenaline flows, and I'm subconsciously getting ready to fight or to run.

Rear Admiral Takijiro Ohnishi, one of Japan's foremost naval aviators, assisted Admiral Yamamoto in the planning of the Pearl Harbor attack. In October of 1944, Ohnishi was a vice admiral in command of the land-based naval air force units remaining in the Philippines after Admiral Halsey's effective assaults.

It was Admiral Ohnishi who instigated the deliberate use of Japan's most dedicated pilots for suicide attacks. He relied in part on the shock effect to disrupt us. In that respect he wasn't far wrong. We had to devise new ways to defend ourselves, and not a few of us had to employ our utmost will not only to fight, but to keep from running right off the ends of the ships in a kind of nautical First Battle of Bull Run.

The kamikazes arrived. It was a whole new war. We had to be constantly on the alert for as many as eighteen raids in a single day. Our fighter cover from the escort carriers at sea did their best, but they could not cut down all the attackers. In Leyte Gulf, almost entirely surrounded by land masses, we were in a box.

There were enemy warships still afloat. The U.S. Army was ashore fighting for Leyte and the Philippines. They had to be supplied with all the war necessities. Troopships were arriving with replacements. Gasoline and oil tankers, ammunition ships, supply ships, tenders — they all had to be protected by the fighters and our umbrella of antiaircraft. We carried on with our gun fire support missions.

Most of the suicide attacks came in the half-light of early morning or late evening, but we learned not to count on it. There was also the "black bitch" — the mid watch from 0000 to 0400 — a nervous time. Eager Japanese pilots would fly around in the dark hoping for some indication of a target — something as small as someone striking a match. It was difficult for us to see them, but they could see us and any fires on board were easy for them to spot. They would try to get at least one hit to start a blaze, then the other planes would head for that ship like buzzards to a carcass.

The first disaster we saw at close hand was the blasting of the cruiser HMAS *Australia*, a great ship, the pride of the Australian Navy. Her sister, HMAS *Canberra*, was sunk at Guadalcanal.

Australia was attacked early one morning. Her guns fired furiously in the semi-darkness while plane after plane dived at her. She was a mass of flame from bow to stern. And through the smoke, the fire, the explosions, the almost continuous thunder of the fleet's heavy guns, punctuated by the intermittent staccato rappings of the light weapons, came over the TBS a calm Aussie voice: "I say, we're being hit a bit . . . ." (*Australia* was subsequently repaired and fought on.)

It was a terrible time. It's one thing to fire on a plane you know will sooner or later pull up and leave. It's quite another when you know it's going to come on in unless it is completely disintegrated. The situation is especially unnerving when your enemy is not only not afraid to die but is actually looking forward to it, an almost incomprehensible attitude that runs counter to every western human instinct.

The officers and men in the directors and on the guns did well, but ship after ship was hit and retired from the scene if the damage was too serious for them to continue.

The bugle calls were our warnings: "Air Defense" was the first to sound when a new raid approached.[1]

---

[1] Buglers stood watch on the bridge. Their calls included: reveille, mess, drill, fire, mail, tattoo, taps and others.

Coming at high volume from every speaker throughout the ship, it snapped everyone to the alert. The first two lines are the Army's "Fix Bayonets." Here's the score:

Air and Torpedo Defense

"General Quarters" followed immediately:

General Quarters.

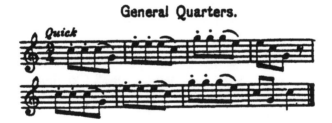

Next, the boatswain's mate of the watch sent his voice through the system: "NOW, ALL HANDS MAN YOUR BATTLE STATIONS; SET MATERIAL CONDITION **ZED**! NOW, ALL HANDS MAN YOUR BATTLE STATIONS; SET MATERIAL CONDITION **ZED**!"

Then the general alarm: "Squawk, squawk, squawk, squawk, squawk . . ." This last went on and on and on and on and on and on, and on!

By then everyone was running at full speed. There were traffic rules to avoid utter chaos with 2,200 officers and men moving in all directions. They were: forward and up the ladders on the starboard side; aft and down on the port side.

It took only two or three minutes to be ready to fight but that could be too long in certain situations. There was devised a partial solution in "condition 1 easy" for the most dangerous periods. This was general quarters, but with ventilation and a few other services provided. All hands were at ease, but readily available at their battle stations. It was, at best, only a makeshift solution as, for example, the 40-mm mounts could not be maintained with their power motors running, in full automatic control from their directors, and with the gun crews standing at their loading stations.

Added to as many as those eighteen raids in a single day mentioned before were false alarms. These arose from friendly aircraft whose identification equipment wasn't working or as a report error from another ship or shore station. The result was an almost continuous alert. Some chose to stay on their battle stations, snatching a nap and a cup of coffee when they could. It wasn't long before most of us showed signs of exhaustion.

Chaplain Sitler and then his relief, Chaplain Francis MacVeigh, carried on with their scheduled and well attended, divine services through all our action periods. Those two bugle calls could interrupt, but the chaplains usually continued when quiet returned.

There were no objections to a two-week break when *Maryland* was ordered back to Manus for rearming, stores, and fuel.

In Seeadler Harbor, Manus, I saw my brother, Paul, for the first time during the war. Five years younger than I, Paul was also a graduate of the Naval Reserve Officers Training Corps at the University of California at Berkeley. *Maryland* had just anchored when a landing craft left a

The USS Talbot *as she appeared just after World War I, before she was converted and designated APD-7. U.S. Naval Photographic Center.*

converted World War I destroyer and raced to our side. There he was with his grin and his head of red hair. Paul was an ensign, a boat officer in the high-speed destroyer transport, USS *Talbot* (APD-7).

Two of *Talbot*'s four boilers had been removed, troop quarters installed, and the mission was fast troop transport, usually at night, and often with underwater demolition teams. The chief duty of the UDTs was to clear the invasion beaches of obstacles to the advance of the assault landing vehicles.

The typical troop transport could not get in and get out fast enough to avoid air attack. Airborne troops could be used, but there was the question of accuracy, especially at night. Destroyer transports filled a definite need.

I had seen what the kamikazes were doing to the destroyer types at Leyte. I knew the entire Philippines were to be retaken. I knew Paul would be leading his two troop-filled landing craft into various contested landing areas. I would have liked to have seen *Talbot* head east with my brother and his little boats.

But in wartime, there are few choices.

Paul invited me to dinner. After meeting his skipper, Commander Francis P. Morgan, USN, his fellow officers, and many of the crew, I felt a little better. It seemed a good ship . . . but it was still a dangerous mission.

Upon our return to Leyte Gulf, it was immediately apparent the Navy was still receiving the concentrated attention of Japan's suicide pilots.

One came over one evening, diving through the clouds at the cruiser *Denver* a short distance to port. From my temporary antiaircraft station on the guns, I saw him fly across a patch of open sky directly above *Maryland*. I could almost read his mind: "Big battleship just below; better target than small cruiser. *Sayonara!*"

Up, over, and into the clouds he zoomed. In a last flurry of bravado he executed some expert final maneuvers, then plunged on, almost straight down towards *Maryland*! Antiaircraft guns can't fire straight up, but all guns that could bear were firing. A tremendous explosion was followed by a roaring ball of flame. I scrambled from the casemate to the deck. Six or eight men emerged from the flames, their clothing on fire, and ran past me, the fully exposed whites of their unseeing eyes contrasted with the blackened faces. That small aircraft, changed by a desperate enemy into a huge and terrible weapon, had missed them by only five to ten feet. They ran a short way down the deck, extinguished their fires, then hastened forward to re-man their guns.

The fire on deck by Turret II diminished in ferocity. We rushed in and removed some of the 20-mm ammunition to prevent a larger fire. There was a popping sound around our feet — like firecrackers. It was exploding ammunition from the aircraft's machine gun.

We remembered HMAS *Australia* and worked desperately to douse the fire as quickly as possible, knowing it served as a beacon for more attacks.

After we thought the fire was out, there is no question we went into a kind of daze. Perhaps it was the sheer awfulness of what had happened. Propeller, airframe, engine, and pilot had disintegrated into hundreds of small

Japanese suicide plane at the moment of impact on Turret II, USS Maryland, Leyte Gulf, November 29, 1944. Author.

pieces, most lying there in the fading light. Our eyes were riveted to the debris. Reputedly, and believably, a man with a long sliver of the plane's metal dragged part of the pilot's head along the deck.

We discovered a burning life raft and threw it over the side. An officer called: "Watch out for your hands!" Too late. The hot tar was burning my fingers.

How could we miss that burning raft? The plane's gasoline had burned itself out. We had stamped out all other burning material. The life raft had been blown from the side of Turret II. Perhaps it landed burning-side down, and the fire finally worked out into the open.

We also did not see until later the round hole in the deck next to the Turret II barbette. Its diameter was only

KAMIKAZE EFFECTIVENESS

The Kamikaze offensives, while they wreaked havoc in the fleets, were often surprisingly impotent. The enemy commanders found it difficult to improve the procedures for two reasons. First, there was never an action report from the principal. Second, the escorting fighters, who were to observe and report the results, were often shot down while protecting their charges.

The kamikazes all carried bombs, but some of the ships hit were not seriously damaged. Those in charge eventually discovered the suicide pilots sometimes neglected to arm their bomb before that final dive. They could not be sent off with the bomb pre-armed, because, should they fail to complete their mission, their return would endanger everyone.

thirteen inches, but the bomb which passed through made all the difference.

Topside damage from the aircraft itself was slight, but the 550-pound bomb had penetrated several decks to an armored deck hatch and exploded. Here it made a large dent with a small slit. Under that sturdy hatch were some of the powder magazines.

The pilot had aimed well. Just a little more speed, and it would been "sayonara" for many more of us.

At Pearl Harbor, *Arizona* had blown up from such a hit. Perhaps we were no longer as objective as we once were, but most of us from then on favored toting around all that heavy steel armor,[2] even if we didn't get there quite as fast.

The amount of damage was still appalling. The bomb's explosion destroyed the sick bay, and all the area

---

[2]   The *Maryland*'s main armored deck was over three inches thick. The side armor was up to sixteen inches, and the turret faces carried eighteen inches.

Damage below decks from kamikaze hit at Leyte Gulf, November 29, 1944. Author.

in the vicinity. Crew's lockers were torn apart, bulkheads blown to pieces and decks obliterated. Thirty-two men were killed and thirty seriously wounded. One poor fellow was found hanging upside down from the overhead with blood running down his face and dripping from his hair. His feet had become wedged between the conduits and the steel structure.

With the operating room demolished, the wounded were tenderly carried by the corpsmen and the mess attendants to the junior and warrant officers' wardrooms. These spaces had been set up as emergency facilities through the foresight of our medical officers.

Several persons involved remarked later on the kind and gentle care received by the wounded, not only from the doctors and the hospital corpsmen whose work it was, but especially from the mess attendants.

Despite our efforts at fire prevention since Pearl Harbor — which included the chipping of all burnable paint to bare metal — there was still a serious fire below decks with heavy smoke. The principal combustibles were bedding and the clothing blown from the metal lockers. Although many of the damage controlmen from that area were among the casualties, fire fighters from other parts of the ship, plus volunteers, efficiently handled the situation. When we became aware of the damage and fire below, we tried to help through a deck hatch, but we had no firemain pressure. The bomb blast had severed the risers.

Maryland left Leyte Gulf three days later, on December 2, 1944, with two badly damaged destroyers as escort. After a brief stop at Manus, we sailed for Pearl Harbor to be repaired.

Bombed at Pearl Harbor, torpedoed at Saipan, and hit by a kamikaze at Leyte, *Maryland* was proving hard to sink. The Japanese had claimed her sunk twice by then, and there was more to come.

The shipyard foremen once again examined our sorely-hit vessel. She was "shot in the belly with an explosive bullet," but she'd live. The "surgeons" operated immediately. With their cutting torches they debrided the crumpled and torn metal in the affected area, which extended over many frames and several decks. The result was a gigantic cavity, and the effect on our visitors was dramatic.

Except for the many air hoses and electrical lines running into every entrance, our exterior appearance was the same as always. When we guided our guests to the midships area, however, they would stop and gasp in astonishment: "What in the devil happened here?" After we told them, "One bomb? Wow!"

One evening we met an Air Force major on his way to Australia. As a result of his friendly mood, which we encouraged after he happened to mention several of his friends who were flight nurses, he wrote the name and Hickam Field telephone number of one nurse on a match book cover.

The next afternoon we conducted a test call. "Well, hello! And how are you?" It was a friendly American-girl voice. She grew even more friendly when we told her we had access to several real steaks, good beer and wine. "OK — come on over." She told us how to find their apartment at Hickam. They lived six in each group.

We talked our cooks out of some choice steaks, brought some beer and a bottle of wine, crawled under the fence to Hickam Field, and knocked on the flight nurses' door. (We might have been able to work our way through the main gate with our dubious naval identification, but we were not as sure of ourselves then as we might be today. Hickam Field was Army Air Force, which was new to us. Hickam was not exactly foreign soil, but we did have a definite sense of adventure as we rose from our dusty stomachs on the Army side of the fence. It's strange to remember how it was before the more or less unified Department of Defense. We actually thought we would probably be jailed if spotted by the military police.)

Our welcome was sincere. Those nurses were wonderful. They broiled steaks and cranked up the pho-nograph. We all ate, drank, danced and had a fine time. Every once in awhile the telephone would ring, then one of the girls would excuse herself and disappear upstairs. She would be right down in her flight gear. A jeep would drive up, and away she would go, to be gone a week, two weeks, who knew? Soon, another jeep would arrive, and a tired young woman would stagger in the door and up the stairs. We wouldn't see her until perhaps the next time we visited.

They were flying the seriously wounded and ill home from New Guinea, the Philippines, wherever, taking those men where they could have the best medical care there was. This was the beginning of a tradition which carried on through the Korean War and Vietnam.

One of the songs played constantly on the wind-up phonograph:

"Give me land, lots of land
Under starry skies above,
Don't fence me in . . ."

Whenever I hear it I still think of those cheerful, hard-working flight nurses. With Amelia Earhart they were in the vanguard of all women who fly — ferry pilots, flight nurses, flight attendants . . . and now, airline pilots and co-pilots, even women in space.

Admiral Raymond Spruance, hero of Midway and the First Battle of the Philippines, came aboard to inspect the damage, as did Admiral Sir Bruce Fraser, RN, victor in his flagship, HMS *Duke of York*, over the German battleship, *Scharnhorst*, and, at the time of his visit, commander of the British Fleet in the Pacific. Damaged ships were not new to either, but we were one of the first home with a kamikaze hit.

When he was well into his retirement years, I met Admiral Spruance. He was polite, quiet, a modest person. Every student of military and naval history knows of the great ones. Theirs are names and deeds called up from memory like treasure. It was an honor and a pleasure to meet an officer who will live forever in the history books.

12

High Flyers

We were pleased to leave the hot tub that was Leyte Gulf, but my feelings were mixed. My brother Paul was going in with his small vessel. There was also my concern for my brother-in-law, Lieutenant Alfred Merrill, who was a B-24 pilot in the Army Air Force's "Jolly Roger Group."

He had been an Air Transport Command navigator but decided he would rather do the driving. His squadron, based at Biak, had been flying in support of the Philippines invasion, and they were soon to move to Mindoro Island, just south of Luzon. "We had to carry maximum loads of gasoline, bombs and ammo for the missions over Formosa and Japanese-controlled China," he said.

Al and his crew were fortunate on their combat missions. Three times they were the only crew in the

B-24 Liberator similar to the type flown by Alfred Merrill of the Jolly Roger Group. Spirits in the Sky.

flight to return to the home strip. The various B-24s they flew were damaged many times, but no one was killed or seriously wounded.

He described two incidents which should be recorded:

As they approached a target on a mission over northern Formosa, an American squadron above suddenly released their full loads of incendiaries. Unbelievably, as if on signal, the planes of Al's squadron, in quick reaction, dived and turned away in all directions. Every one of the hundreds of small bombs missed the aircraft of his squadron!

Another target was a railroad bridge on the coast of China across the South China Sea from the Philippines. As Al's group was pulling away from their bomb run, they noted a single Japanese Zero fighter taking off from a strip near the bridge. One of the crewmen suggested over the interphone:

"Let's get a Zero!"

Al shoved the throttles forward and put the aircraft into a steep dive after the unsuspecting fighter. At maximum speed with the dual tail fins quivering, they closed

What they were after: the Mitsubishi A6M5 Reisen or Japanese "Zero."
Spirits in the Sky.

until the gunners could open with all the forward-firing guns.

"Let him have it!" Al said over the phones.

There were many hits with pieces of the plane flying off, but it kept going.

The Japanese pilot dived for the ground and followed a railroad track along the coast. The chase ended when antiaircraft guns guarding a bridge shot out two of Al's engines. There they were: "on the deck," short of gas, and many miles from home.

During the long journey over the South China Sea, they searched for updrafts in thunderheads to give them additional lift and everything they didn't need went overboard to lighten the load. They were greatly relieved when they sighted their home strip and made a safe landing long after dark.

13

OKINAWA
ONSLAUGHT

S hipshape again, and loaded, *Maryland* had six days
of firing and drills off Kahoolawe Island, then sailed
for Ulithi in the Caroline Islands to witness a sight
which probably will never be seen again. The U.S. fleet
at Ulithi would have filled most of San Francisco Bay:
hundreds of ships of all types, including fleet carriers, escort
carriers, new and old battleships, cruisers, destroyers, landing craft, command ships, transports, tankers, cargo ships,
tenders, ammunition ships, minelayers, minesweepers, fleet
rescue tugs . . .

It was a stupendous congregation of vessels which
stretched over the horizon and over the horizon's horizon.

Hidden in that mass of ships was one special to me
— USS *Talbot*. And again, as soon as we anchored, a
small boat sped our way bearing that grinning young ensign,

my brother Paul. He was a combat veteran now, taking troops into Lingayen Gulf, Bataan, and Corregidor. His skipper had successfully dodged every kamikaze that happened by.

They had a scenic trip through the Philippines. Paul talked about the sunsets. But these were not the brilliant panoramas pictured on postcards. "The clouds were tinted various shades of red from the glow of burning and exploding ships."

"Tell me about the landings, Paul."

"There was Lingayen Gulf on Luzon Island first. We were in the boats heading for the beach when an LCM (Landing Craft, Medium) hit a mine and blew up. We were just behind, but had no problem. It was not the usual way to clear a channel, but it worked.

"Toward the end of February (1945), Ensign James from New York City and I took our four boats loaded with combat troops into a landing on the southwest tip of Bataan at Mariveles Bay. Several of the captured American 9-inch guns on Corregidor opened fire. Big splashes, but we were moving and turning so fast, those gunners just couldn't keep up with us. We had ordered the troops to stay low in the boats, but one soldier had to see what was going on. A near miss removed his head. It was our only casualty.

"That night, *Talbot* was ordered on a high-speed run north to Subic Bay (Luzon Island) to load paratroopers (of the Army's 503rd Regimental Combat Team)."

It was planned to drop the entire team on the parade ground and golf course Topside on Corregidor, but a rising wind forced the diversion of several units to the high-speed transports.

Ensign James and Paul were soon engaged in landing *Talbot*'s new load of troops on a small beach at the base of Corregidor's cliffs. Defending that island were 5,200 well-supplied Japanese troops in superb condition.

All was quiet, however, until just before the moment of landing.

"Suddenly, the entire beach and adjacent areas erupted with perfectly aimed Japanese mortar fire," Paul said. "Our wooden boats were well-splintered, and the troops were quite willing to disembark and wade ashore in the shallow water.

"We were in trouble as we withdrew and turned to get out of range. At this critical moment, a destroyer[1] charged in between our boats and the cliff with all guns firing at point-blank range. It was a sight to see!"

On Mog Mog Island in Ulithi, Paul and I were sitting on a coconut log, and I was feeling sorry for all the people in the world who have never had a brother. We were happy and warmed by the sun. The beach sand was the purest white. The sky and the sea displayed those beautiful shades of clean and transparent blue.

"Paul, with all those suicide planes, how did the *Talbot* manage to escape?"

"Our skipper's getting real good at it now," Paul said. "As soon as air defense goes, and there are 'bandits' in the air, our captain goes to work with 'all engines ahead, flank!' It was always flank, and more than flank. He asked the engineers for every turn they could give. It was one of his theories that the pilot up there would tend to disregard a slim, fast-moving and turning small target in favor of one large and not quite so speedy."

Paul was pensively studying good old *Maryland* riding at anchor close by. She was presenting her starboard quarter just then. I reassured him as to *Maryland*'s unusual speed and maneuverability.

---

[1] USS *Claxton* (DD-571), Commander M. H. Hubbard. She was also the flagship of our battle line's destroyer screen during the Battle of Surigao Strait. She reported a 14-inch shell's near-miss at Surigao.

While drinking his beer, Paul explained his captain's belief that the typical Japanese kamikaze pilot was understandably nervous.

"For sure, he had never killed himself before. He was fanatically committed to this act, but he was still human. At the start of that final dive, thoughts of home and family could crowd in. *That* was the time to trick him. We hoped he was up there daydreaming."

Sitting there in safety, we laughed at this fantasy, but it turned out Commander Morgan was, in more than a few cases, not far off. Some of the suicide pilots' failure to arm their bombs has already been mentioned. Some dived so fast, their controls froze, and they could not make the necessary last-second corrections. At 350 knots they would travel almost the length of two football fields in one second! No blinking, no heavy breathing, not too fast, hand on throttle, hand on stick . . . total attention to duty through the last split second . . . the kamikaze pilot's mission required almost superhuman concentration.

We knew when we entered Ulithi that massive concentration of ships indicated a huge operation was coming up, but we didn't know where. It was only after we got underway that we were told our objective was Okinawa. This island was a part of Japan's homeland. The enemy would immediately realize we would use it as a base for the invasion of their main islands and would defend it fiercely. We would have to perform with the greatest efficiency if *Maryland* were to survive.

Maryland would provide fire support for the Okinawa campaign. In Task Force 54, under Vice Admiral Morton L. Deyo, in *Tennessee,* were ten old battleships: USS *Arkansas* (BB-33), USS *New York* (BB-34), USS *Texas* (BB-35), USS *Nevada* (BB-36), USS *New Mexico*

(BB-40), USS *Idaho* (BB-42), USS *Tennessee* (BB-43), USS *Colorado* (BB-45), USS *Maryland* (BB-46) and USS *West Virginia* (BB-48) plus many cruisers and destroyers.

ARKANSAS AND NEW YORK

Old *Arkansas* with her 12-inch guns! Her keel was laid in 1909 by New York Shipbuilding, Camden, N. J. She served with Britain's Grand Fleet during World War I, supported the invasions of Normandy and southern France in 1944, and bombarded Cherbourg. A sacrificial target for the Bikini A-bomb tests, she remained afloat after the July 1, 1946 test; the second bomb, July 25th, finally sent her under.

New York supported the landings in North Africa and helped destroy French battleship *Jean Bart* at Casablanca to prevent her from coming under control of the Germans. During the war *New York* steamed 123,667 nautical miles and was in action 414 days. After the war she survived both atom bomb tests and eventually had to be scuttled near Hawaii in 1948.

USS New York *(BB-34) as she appeared in 1915, three years after launching. National Archives.*

USS *Mississippi* (BB-41) arrived at Okinawa on April 20 and USS *California* (BB-44) arrived on June 15. Most of the ten new battleships, USS *North Carolina* (BB-55), USS *Washington* (BB-56), USS *South Dakota* (BB-57), USS *Indiana* (BB-58), USS *Massachusetts* (BB-59), USS *Alabama* (BB-60), USS *Iowa* (BB-61), USS *New Jersey* (BB-62), USS *Missouri* (BB-63), USS *Wisconsin* (BB-64); the two new 12-inch battle cruisers, USS *Alaska* (CB-1) and USS *Guam* (CB-2), and several British ships bombarded Okinawa before we arrived.

A friend, Russell Terrell, was an Army sergeant in the 383rd Amphibious Assault Team at Okinawa. He told me they built ladders to mount an eleven-foot sea wall the Japanese had constructed to prevent typhoon wave damage. He said: "We didn't need the ladders because the *King George V* went in and blew the sea wall apart!"

BATTLESHIP RECIPROCATING ENGINES

Two of our old battleships had steam reciprocating engines. *Texas* and *New York* loyally cranked themselves over to Europe for the landings then, back, down through the Panama Canal, and on out to Okinawa. That is cranking! *Arkansas* completed the same voyage, but she had four turbines.

Admiral Deyo brought much experience to these operations. He commanded the fire support ships at Utah Beach in the Normandy landings and at Cherbourg. *Texas, Arkansas*, and *Nevada* were all useful there and in other areas. *Nevada* delivered some brilliant fire which was requested by airborne troops deep in Normandy's interior. The target was a German tank formation, and the range was fourteen miles. Imagine the consternation of the German tankers in those pre-guided-missile days when they realized they were being hit by major caliber (14-inch) shells so far inland. *Texas* took a hit from an 11-inch gun at Cherbourg and helped in the destruction of one of the four guns of that battery.

Maryland's new commanding officer, Captain J. D. Wilson, continued with many drills enroute to Okinawa, and there was occasion for expert ship handling as we fueled the destroyers at sea during heavy weather.

For Okinawa and other operations the Navy had developed a radar picket destroyer system. These moved out from the fire support ships and transports and were able to give earlier air raid warnings. They usually had fighter director officers aboard who could point the combat air patrol toward the incoming enemy both as to direction and distance. Some of the picket ships had advanced radars which could determine the kamikaze attackers' altitudes. This, obviously, was a tremendous advantage. It was no surprise when these outlying ships became choice targets. On the first day our picket was badly hit and sinking. Another destroyer steamed to her rescue and was sunk.

The kamikaze raids were almost continuous, and ship after ship was seriously damaged or sunk. Some of the radar picket destroyers were hit by as many as thirty suicide planes, one after the other — sometimes in groups!

The order would be sent to a close screening ship to replace a damaged picket. "Wilco," (will comply) would be the cheerful response on the TBS radio. There would be that puff of black smoke from one of the screen, she would heel over in a hard turn, and head at high speed over the horizon. The "small boys" were admired by the big ship crews. We couldn't do enough for them in the way of ice cream and such when they came alongside.

Maryland had her share of satisfactions. One day, the cruiser *Minneapolis* uncovered shore batteries on the island's west side while we were on the east side firing on enemy positions. We promptly steamed down and around to the west. Our 16-inch guns soon eliminated the Japanese positions.

HUGH W. HADLEY (DD774)

USS Hugh W. Hadley *(DD-774) in dazzle paint.   U.S. Naval Photographic Center.*

The destroyers were heroes of the fleet. A Presidential unit citation to USS *Hugh W. Hadley* (DD774), the destroyer in which 1942 NROTC classmate Lieutenant Hunter S. Robbins, Jr. served, tells the story:

THE SECRETARY OF THE NAVY
Washington

The President of the United States takes pleasure in presenting the PRESIDENTIAL UNIT CITATION to the UNITED STATES SHIP HUGH W. HADLEY for service as set forth in the following CITATION:

"For extraordinary heroism, in action as Fighter Direction Ship on Radar Picket Station Number 15 during an attack by approximately 100 enemy Japanese planes, forty miles northwest of the Okinawa Transport Area, May 11, 1945. Fighting valiantly against waves of hostile suicide and dive-bombing planes plunging toward her from all directions, the U.S.S. HUGH W. HADLEY sent up relentless barrages of antiaircraft fire during one of the most furious air-sea battles of the war. Repeatedly finding her targets, she destroyed twenty enemy planes, skillfully directed her Combat Air Patrol in shooting down at least forty others and, by her vigilance and superb battle readiness, avoided damage to herself until subjected to a coordinated attack by ten Japanese planes.

Assisting in the destruction of all ten of these, she was crashed by one bomb and three suicide planes with devastating effect. With all engineering spaces flooded and with a fire raging amidships, the gallant officers and men of the HUGH W. HADLEY fought desperately against almost insurmountable odds and, by their indomitable determination, fortitude and skill, brought the damage under control, enabling their ship to be towed to port and saved. Her brilliant performance in this action reflects the highest credit upon the HUGH W. HADLEY and the United States Naval Service."

For the President,

(signed) James Forrestal

Secretary of the Navy

Maryland also had her share of frustrations. Our observation pilot of Tarawa fame, Lieutenant Whaley, spotted a Japanese tank, buried so just its turret and gun were exposed. He called in the target, and it was assigned to the secondary battery, port side — my battery. This was a very small object to hit — a circle perhaps three feet in diameter with a short pipe extending from one side and it was miles away near the brow of a hill.

We would send out a four-gun salvo and give Lt. Whaley a warning "splash" from our time-of-flight clock. He would wing over and spot our bursts as they landed. "No change, no change, I guess," from Mr. Whaley after a few spotting salvos.

Here was a situation as illustrated by the chart on page 98. After we got on in range and bearing (deflection), a short shell of a straddling salvo could land just in front of the target. A long shell in that same salvo could miss just over the top of the tank turret and fly on for hundreds of yards. The observer, looking down from above, might see three bursts around the target and the fourth burst a quarter-mile away.

"Some straddle!"

We were on, however, in range and bearing, and we could do no better than that. We fired for effect, but no hits. The tank was within the spread of our shell bursts. The odds would sooner or later have given us a hit, but our spotting plane could not stay there forever. Minus that hit, "brown shoe" Whaley joshed "black shoe" Sauer for the rest of the war.[2]

We conducted a simulated bombardment and landing at Okinawa's south end in an effort to draw some of the enemy away from the actual landing areas. Perhaps Admiral Deyo chose *Maryland*, a 16-inch gunned ship, for the duty to convince Japanese naval observers ashore that here, since the largest guns were being used, was indeed the site for an important assault. Similar ruses were effective in Europe.

The suicide air attacks continued. After a hurried dinner one evening in a lull between the raids, a small black mess attendant said, "I want to be on the guns. I can hit 'em good. I know I can."

Standing by the door, I stared at him. He looked me straight in the eye. I knew I was looking at a warrior. I thought, we are fighting for a country in which there is a chance we eventually could be an example to the world. All people could live together without trying to annihilate one another. Perhaps that is our mission!

An automatic weapons officer agreed with me and assigned that man to a 20-mm antiaircraft gun. My regret is that I didn't follow through to see where he was and

---

[2] Naval aviators were authorized to wear green uniforms. Black shoes did not go well with that color, so they had brown shoes. These shoes also went well with the khakis we all wore, so the aviators wore their brown shoes with their khakis. The rest of us did not have brown shoes, so we — proudly — wore black shoes with khakis.

how he did. I've often wondered if his battle station was at or near our final hit.

Everyone stationed there surely remembers the nights in the tops off Okinawa.

When there was little wind, the ships would lie in a fairly close group so the destroyers and other vessels could make smoke and cover us all. On those smoke nights there would be two situations: The thick smoke would cover us completely, or the smoke would be thick enough, but not deep enough. In the latter case the small ships would be nicely hidden, and so would the big ships, except for the foretops! There we would sit, protruding from that grey blanket, like mid-channel obstruction markers.

"Here we are. Here's one of the big fellas. Come on over and dump on us!"

But on the night remembered, we were completely covered. With nothing visible from above, the Japanese responded by flying back and forth in the smoke until they hit something.

We could hear them as we lay doggo. Not a shot could we fire.

Suddenly, a plane burst out of the smoke to starboard, a little forward of the beam, and roared over just aft and a little up. As he passed, and before he almost instantly disappeared on the port quarter, he released five or six parachute flares. They settled toward the water on both sides as we foretopmen stared at each other in the eerie yellow light they cast.

For a change of pace, the Japanese command ordered out that nightmare antagonist, 18.1" *Yamato*, the light cruiser, *Yahagi*, and a destroyer squadron on a suicide run. In what promised to be a spectacular finish, they were to beach themselves at Okinawa and expend all their ammunition.

All we knew then, of course, was that they were at sea, so on April 7, 1945, the old battleships again formed in line of battle. Our commander was Admiral Deyo. Careful preparations for surface action were completed as we steamed north to engage.

Just before dusk a plane came down the line to starboard and dived on us. *Maryland* was the last in column, so it was the pilot's final opportunity to catch a big one.

We opened with everything. The mass of bright tracers going into the darkness marked a seemingly impenetrable wall of fire. The hundreds of tracers also made it extremely difficult for the director operators and gunners to track the incoming target.

The kamikaze came on and on. Pieces of the plane were shot off, but that pilot steered her right on in, and his craft with its bomb exploded with a horrendous flash on top of Turret III. The 20-mm gunners stationed on top of that turret fired until the end. All but one died; we lost seventeen men with thirty-seven wounded.

Justin J. David of Shreveport, Louisiana, was the lone survivor from the top of Turret III. I met him at *Maryland*'s reunion, September, 1994, in San Diego. "Yes, I was the gunner on a twenty millimeter. I shot at him and I remember hitting him. No, I don't remember being hit by him but I was still shooting. They found my gun barrel, bent, with a shell stuck in it."

The bomb from the crashed plane exploded on the turret top not more than five feet away from David, probably closer!

Maryland was one of 368 ships damaged at Okinawa. Twenty-six ships were sunk, 4,900 officers and

Above, Japanese suicide plane approaching starboard side of Maryland, *Okinawa, April 7, 1945. Center photo shows the moment of impact and the lower photo, just after.   U.S. Navy.*

Suicide plane hit, top of Turret III, Okinawa, April 7, 1945. Dent in armor at left is site of bomb explosion. All but one of the gunners atop the turret died; the ninety men inside survived. Author.

men killed and almost as many wounded. Those numbers — twenty-six sunk and 368 damaged, totalling 394 — are so hard to visualize, they have no real meaning. Imagine yourself on the Golden Gate Bridge and watching a ghostly parade of 394 ships in column standing up the main ship channel and passing underneath. At 500-yard intervals, when the first steams under, the last will be ninety-eight nautical miles at sea!

Yamato, Yahagi and four of the eight destroyers were sunk by more than 300 aircraft from the Task Force 38 carriers.

We were in a situation at Okinawa similar to that in Leyte Gulf, only probably more difficult because of our proximity to the airstrips on the Japanese home islands, on

Formosa, and even in China. Our people on the beach at Okinawa needed, as always, heavy fire support. The vulnerable supply ships required constant antiaircraft protection.

Old *New York* was in action at Okinawa for 76 days. She fired more than 11,000 rounds of 14-inch and 5-inch and was slightly damaged by a suicide plane on April 14th.

Her sister, *Texas*, stayed and fought for 89 days.

Nevada operated at Okinawa from March 25th to June 30th — 94 days. She was hit March 27th by a kamikaze, and on April 5th by a shore battery.

New Mexico came on April 1st and remained until May 12th, when she was hit and took moderate damage. On April 12th she splashed four planes in sixteen minutes.

In a lighter moment, DiMartino, GM3/c, fifth Div. poses with wise young owl that underwent bombardment at Okinawa until he decided to fly out to the safer end of the gun. Author.

USS New Mexico *(BB-40) anchored off Mt. Fujiyama, Japan shortly after the war.   U.S. Naval Photographic Center.*

Mississippi arrived on April 20th and was hit on June 5th with slight damage. As reported, she was a "sharpshooter." Near the end of May, *Mississippi* fired 1,300 14-inch shells at heavily fortified Shuri Castle — the Japanese headquarters on Okinawa — and destroyed it.

Idaho fought from March 25th to April 20th, but was hit on April 12th by aerial torpedoes. She was repaired and returned to her Okinawa fire support mission on May 22nd.

Tennessee suffered a hit on April 12th, but stayed and fought for 91 days.

California was there June 15th to July 21st after being repaired from her hit at Lingayen Gulf.

Our sister ship, *Colorado*, furnished fire support at Okinawa from April 1st to May 22nd and again in August.

Our other sister ship, *West Virginia*, served at Okinawa from April 1st to June 17th. She was hit by a kamikaze on her first day there and bombed on June 17th with moderate damage on both occasions.

Arkansas arrived at Okinawa on March 25th, suffered no hits, and returned to the States in October, 1945. *Maryland's* final days will be recorded in the coming pages.

All the other ships contributed their fair share at Okinawa, and it would be a pleasure to list their accomplishments. There were, however, over 1,200 vessels involved. We must, therefore, be content here with the

USS California *(BB-44) after being modernized at Bremerton. The dazzle paint was replaced with battleship gray by the time the events at Okinawa occurred. National Archives.*

stories of *Maryland* and the other tenacious, almost indestructible old battleships.

The saga of the fleet that wouldn't leave is a glorious chapter in American, British, and Australian naval history. The battle for Okinawa was the longest, hardest of any in the Pacific since Guadalcanal. According to Samuel E. Morison, "Naval gunfire was employed longer and in greater quantities in the Battle of Okinawa than in any other in history." It was the end of the Japanese fleet. At Okinawa, the Allied forces finished the job begun at Surigao.

14

VICTORIOUS

Our orders were to proceed to Puget Sound Naval Shipyard for repair and modernization. Modernization? This late in the war? There could be only one reason: we were going to Japan and Admirals King and Nimitz foresaw the need for every possible fire support ship. Iwo Jima and Okinawa made it plain that the Japanese defense of their home islands would be utterly ferocious.

We were soon involved in the hustle of the yard availability at Bremerton. *West Virginia, Tennessee, California*, and other ships had already been repaired and gone through the modernization process. The work progressed rapidly.

All the 5-inch 51-caliber and 5-inch 25-caliber guns were landed. They were replaced by eight dual-purpose 5-

The author about 1950.   Author.

inch 38-caliber twin mounts with their two radar-equipped Mark 37 directors. The new secondary battery plotting room was installed near main battery plot below the armored decks.

We received all new electronics and other fire control equipment. Worn machinery was overhauled or replaced. The bottom was cleaned and painted. Bunks replaced hammocks and cots.

Thirty-day leaves were granted to all hands, and Captain Wilson authorized the maximum number of overnight liberties to those not on leave.

Officers and men of the watch on duty underwent the traditional chaos of shipboard life in a shipyard.

The continuing racket in a steel ship has to be experienced to be believed. Sounds carry into every compartment. The cutting and welding is fairly quiet, although the fumes go everywhere. Air hammers are used for some work; there is much movement of heavy equipment, crunches, tools dropped, shouted orders. There are many debates between shipyard people and ship's personnel about what goes where and how it is to be installed.

Yard work was completed on schedule. On August 15, 1945, just as we left for Southern California to train for the invasion of Japan, the Japanese surrendered.

Knowing what we did about the Japanese defenses and their determination, we were all relieved that President

Truman's decision to use the atomic bomb had hastened Japan's capitulation.

We in the ships facing the kamikazes, and our brothers on the islands battling the Japanese defenders, learned to respect the sheer courage and the skill of the Japanese fighting men. Had the war continued, and if we were forced to invade Japan, there can be no doubt there would have been hundreds and hundreds of thousands of Americans and Japanese dead, or maimed, to the lasting sorrow of all the survivors.

Another factor most certainly entered into the A-bomb decision. That was the terrible plight of the Allied prisoners of war held by the Japanese. When the Philippines were liberated, news confirming the Bataan Death March, and other atrocities, reached our high command.

Gavan Daws in his 1994 book, *Prisoners of the Japanese*, details the horrible conditions: the beatings, the starvation, the disease, the scarcities of medical service, sanitation facilities, and clothing. He wrote that of the 140,000 American, British, Australian, and Dutch military prisoners, twenty-seven percent were dead at the war's end. A year more of warfare would probably have resulted in the deaths of most of those in the home islands and in other non-liberated areas.

OLYMPIC, code-name for the planned November 1st invasion of the Kyushu beaches around Kagoshima and Ariake, had been anticipated accurately by Japanese intelligence. According to William Craig in his book, *The Fall of Japan*, published in 1967, an operational defense plan called KETSU-GO was circulating through the Japanese Navy and Army general staffs. Five thousand, two hundred twenty-five planes were to be used as kamikazes against the American troop transports and the supporting vessels at the landing beaches — Kagoshima and Ariake! By analysis of our radio traffic and by other means, their intelligence estimated that November 1st would be the invasion date. The Japanese would have been in place and ready to defend their homeland to the last man.

Following is a quote from Emperor Hirohito lmperial Rescript of August 15, 1945, in which he directed the Japanese people to surrender:

> Moreover, the enemy has begun to employ a new and most cruel bomb, the power of which to do damage is indeed incalculable, taking the toll of many innocent lives. Should we continue to fight, it would not only result in an ultimate collapse and obliteration of the Japanese nation, but also it would lead to the total extinction of human civilization.

President Truman will go down in history as a brave and able man who did not hedge in his terrible choice of the lesser of two immeasurable evils.

There we were, modernized and qualified for combat, but, happily, no more combat, so *Maryland* was converted to the work of a troop transport. We carried our people home on the glorious "Magic Carpet" duty. It is difficult to adequately describe the overjoyed reactions of our war veteran passengers as we churned through the entrance channels to San Francisco and San Diego. Our most memorable trip was from Hawaii to San Diego with five hundred happy homeward bounders.

Maryland was the first battleship into San Diego's harbor in many years, and our reception was magnificent. As we moored to the downtown Navy Peir, we were greeted by well over five thousand people. A band played and Dinah Shore sang. Later, she came aboard for breakfast, much to everyone's delight.

USS Maryland *(BB-46) as she appeared April 26, 1944. National Archives.*

The United States Navy's third *Maryland* completed her active duty career in 1946. She was mothballed at Bremerton, and, sadly, scrapped at San Pedro, California in 1959.

It was an honor and a privilege to serve aboard USS *Maryland*.

GLOSSARY
APPENDICES
BIBLIOGRAPHY
INDEX

BATTLESHIP GLOSSARY

At the Dip. A signal flag hoist attached to the halyard but flown partway down, usually in anticipation of acknowledging an order from the flagship.

Barbette. An armored cylinder that protects the lower part of a turret.

Barrage. An overwhelming quantity of artillery fire.

Battery. A group of guns having the same caliber or used for the same purpose.

Beach. Used to refer to anyplace ashore. "I had two weeks leave so I spent it on the beach."

Bombardment. A vigorous attack with primary and secondary batteries of several ships.

Breech. The opening and mechanism at the rear part of the bore of a gun that allows for insertion of the projectile.

Brow. A short gangplank used to get from one ship to another or ashore. Used when there is little vertical difference from one to the other.

Casemates.   The lightly armored enclosures around the broadside guns.

Director, Fire Control.   Mechanical and/or electronic device used to keep a ship's guns on target taking into account variables such as target movement, own vessel course and speed, wind, etc.

Doubled.   Mooring lines are doubled when the end of the line goes ashore and back to the ship, thus doubling the strength (and length) of the line.

Enfiladed.   A military position, such as a trench, subject to sweeping fire from one end to the other by the enemy.

Execute.   In battleship maneuvers, when each ship understands and is ready to comply with an order sent by signal flag, she two-blocks or raises her flag hoist all the way up, beginning with the end ships of each division.   After all hoists are two-blocked, the flagship hauls her hoist down, which action is followed by all the others.   This is the signal to execute.

Fire Control.   The center for controlling weapons fire on a ship.   Fire control, in effect, aims the ship's weapons at the enemy, allowing for wind, speed, location, range, altitude, etc.

Fusillade.   A simultaneous or continuous discharge of weapons.

GQ, General Quarters.   The condition of readiness when attack is imminent.   All hands are required to be at their stations in lifejackets and battle helmets.

Ground Tackle.   The equipment used to anchor a ship: anchors, chain, windlass and appurtenances.

Pointer.   The person on a naval gun who brings the gun to the proper elevation.

Redoubled.   A ship's lines are redoubled when the end of the line is sent to the dock, returned to the ship, sent to the dock again and returned to the ship again; in other words quadrupled.

Seaman's Eye. A person who has several years of experience uses his "seaman's eye" to arrive at the same conclusion someone else might achieve through lengthy and time-consuming calculation.

Steaming Colors. The American Flag flown on the steaming gaff (on the after mast) while at sea. In port, the flag is flown from the stern.

TBS. Talk Between Ships. A line-of-sight radio system used when ships are relatively close to one another.

Two-blocked. A flag raised to the top of the halyard.

Trainer. The person on a naval gun who adjusts the horizontal direction of fire.

Turret. A low, heavily armored structure which revolves horizontally and contains large caliber guns.

Zed.[1] The material condition which prepares a ship for battle by achieving the utmost in watertight integrity. All watertight doors and hatches are closed, most ventilation secured and the ship is otherwise prepared to minimize flooding and the spread of fire in the event of battle damage.

---

[1] During World War II "Zed" was the International Code word for the letter Z. This was later changed to "Zebra."

Appendix A

Loading a 16-inch Gun

Following is a description of the loading proce-dures in a 16-inch battleship turret. It was written in 1994 by Fleet A. Hamby of Port Orchard, Washington. Hamby served as a Gunners Mate First Class in Turret II aboard Maryland.

Since there are no longer any battleships in com-mission this account is of considerable historical impor-tance:

Duties of Loading Crew for 16-Inch 45-Caliber Main Battery Gun

With the previously fired gun at load position, and on order of *turret officer*, "load," the *plugman* (*gun cap-tain*) disengages the salvo latch and pushes it all the way down. This rotates the breech plug which is then forced down against counter balance springs and latched open by the stiff leg mechanism.

When the plug is latched in down position, the primerman, who stands on a lower platform down and under the gun, inserts the primer into the firing lock. The primerman must be tall, six feet, or more.

The left gun *plugman* has three layers of toweling, kept wet, wrapped around his right arm from wrist to elbow. (The right gun *plugman* would have his left arm wrapped.) The arm is wiped over the mushroom to cool it and to wipe away any burning particles that may be on the mushroom.

The *plugman* then determines if the "bore is clear." He is assisted by the "gas ejection air" that was turned on when the salvo latch was opened and the plug rotated the first three to four inches. The gas ejection air ports are evenly spaced around the inside of breech.

The *trayman* then lowers the tray, which spans the distance from loading platform into the gun powder chamber. A lip is fashioned in the forward end of tray. It has approximately six inches of movement forward to further extend the tray. This lip is extended while loading but must be in the aft, or retract, position to lower or raise the tray.

With the bore clear and the tray lip forward, the *plugman* gives a hand signal to the *rammerman* to ram the projectile. The rammer, powered by an electrohydraulic motor, forces the projectile along the tray, through the powder chamber, and hard into the bore. The copper rotating band around the projectile's base is firmly seated in the rifling. The rammerman retracts the rammer to the loading platform and waits for *plugman* and *trayman* to unload the powder car onto the tray.

The powder car has a false bottom that is spring loaded. It has been loaded in the upper powder handling room with five powder bags, on their sides, on three levels. There is a stack of three in the car's forward end, and a stack of two aft. The *plugman* and the *trayman* lean over the tray and unlatch tht flameproof powder car door. The door slides down; exposes the first bag at tray level. The *plugman* rolls it onto the tray and shoves it forward into the gun powder chamber. The *powder car operator* raises the false bottom, bringing two more bags up to the tray level. The *plugman* rolls one onto the tray and pushes it forward. The *trayman* rolls the other bag onto the tray and pushes it aft. The *powder car operator* raises the last two bags to tray level. The *plugman* rolls out the forward bag, and the *trayman* rolls out the aft bag. They close the powder car door, and the car is returned to the upper powder handling room to be reloaded.

With the powder bags on the tray, the *rammerman gently* gathers them together with his rammer and shoves them into the powder chamber. The rammer is then fully withdrawn, and another projectile is rolled into position in front of the rammer head.

With the rammer withdrawn, the *plugman* retracts the tray lip; the *trayman* lifts the tray to the upright position and steps back off the movable loading platform attached to the underside of the gun. The *plugman* trips the stiff leg by a foot pedal, which releases the plug. He then turns on air pressure to assist in closing the plug. As the plug closes, it is cammed to rotate clockwise approximately twenty-five degrees. The *plugman* will then, by hand, raise the salvo latch. He follows it to the fully latched position. This action locks the breach closed, so that it cannot be accidently opened before the round is fired. The *plugman* then steps off the movable platform and turns on his ready light. This tells the *turret officer* the gun is ready to be aimed and fired.

In Turret II aboard *Maryland*, our crews could complete this entire loading procedure in about fifteen seconds, sometimes faster.

Appendix B

The Demise
of the
Old Battlewagon

Alabama was stricken on June 1, 1962 and became a war memorial on January 9, 1965.

Arkansas was a target for the atom bomb tests in 1946. She remained afloat after the first test. The second bomb, July 25, sent her to the bottom.

California operated in the South China Sea after Okinawa. On October 15, 1945, she and *Tennessee* were ordered the long way home, from Japan around the world via Singapore-Colombo-Cape Town to Philadelphia. It was an unusual voyage then, but a happy one as a representative of the victorious Allies. Placed in reserve and then mothballs at Philadelphia, *California* was scrapped beginning March, 1960, at Baltimore.

Colorado was placed in reserve, then mothballs, and scrapped beginning July, 1959, at Seattle after being towed from her mooring at Bremerton.

185

Idaho was scrapped beginning December 12, 1947, at Newark, New Jersey.

Indiana was sold for scrap on September 6, 1963.

Iowa was reactivated from 1951 to 1958 and again from 1983 to 1990. She was stricken on January 13, 1995 and is being offered as a museum.

Massachusetts was stricken on June 1, 1962 and became a war memorial at Fall River on August 14, 1965.

Maryland was mothballed in 1946. She was scrapped at San Pedro, California, in 1959.

After the war, *Mississippi* was converted to a gunnery and guided missile test ship and not scrapped until December 7, 1956, at Baltimore.

Missouri remained active to 1954 and was reactivated from 1986 to 1992. She was stricken on January 13, 1995 and currently is at Pearl Harbor undergoing restoration as a museum.

Nevada, like *New York,* survived both atom bomb tests at Bikini. She was then used as a target vessel and survived gunfire from 16-inch *Iowa* and several cruisers. *Nevada* was finally sunk on July 31, 1948, by an aerial torpedo.

New Jersey was active from 1950 to 1957, 1967 to 1969 and 1982 to 1981. She was stricken on January 13, 1995 and is being offered as a museum.

New Mexico was decommissioned in Boston, July 19, 1946, and broken up at Newark, N. J., beginning November 27, 1947.

New York survived both atom bomb tests. She was scuttled near Hawaii in 1948.

North Carolina was stricken June 1, 1960 and became a war memorial on April 29, 1962.

Oklahoma was sold for scrap on December 5, 1946 and sank under tow, 540 miles NE of Pearl Harbor on May 17, 1947

May 24, 1986, sailors of the USS New Jersey *line the rail as they prepare to render honors as the battlehips passes the* Arizona *Memorial at Pearl Harbor, Hawaii.   U.S. Navy.*

Pennsylvania, due to damage in the Philippines, did not participate in the Okinawa operation.   She survived both Bikini bomb tests and was scuttled on February 10, 1948.

South Dakota was sold for scrap on October 25, 1962.

After the war *Tennessee* was in mothballs at Philadelphia until she was scrapped in Baltimore from July, 1959.

From 1941 to 1945 *Texas*, commissioned December 3. 1914, fought 116 actions, steamed 121,000 miles, and fired 4,278 14-inch shells.   The citizens of Texas gained the respect of us battleship sailors when it was learned in 1948 that they were berthing *Texas* as a permanent memorial and war museum near their famed battleground of San Jacinto.   Texans could give battleship *Texas* no greater honor because it was at San Jacinto that their General Sam Houston defeated Mexico's General Santa Anna and established Texas's independence.

Mothballed at Bremerton, *West Virginia* was scrapped at Seattle beginning January, 1961.

Washington was sold for scrap on May 24, 1961.

Wisconsin was reactivated from 1951 to 1958 and 1988 to 1991. She was stricken on January 13, 1995 and is being offered as a museum.

Appendix C

American
Battleship
Directory

Compiled by: Bill Navobdaky, Hopewell, New Jersey
Reprinted courtesy ALNAVCO LOG

Hull No.	Name	Length	Displace-ment	Keel Laid	Commis-sioned	Main Armament
2nd line	*Texas*	308' 10"	6,315	6-1-89	8-15-95	2x12"
2nd line	*Maine*	319'	6,682	10-17-89	9-17-95	4x10"
BB-1	*Indiana*	350' 11"	10,288	5-17-91	11-20-95	4x13"
BB-2	*Massachusetts*	350' 11"	10,288	6-25-91	6-10-96	4x13"
BB-3	*Oregon*	351' 1/2"	10,288	11-19-91	7-15-96	4x13"
BB-4	*Iowa*	362' 5"	11,410	8-5-93	6-16-97	4x12"
BB-5	*Kearsarge*	375' 4"	11,540	6-30-96	2-20-00	4x13"
BB-6	*Kentucky*	375' 4"	11,540	6-30-96	5-15-00	4x13"
BB-7	*Illinois*	375' 4"	11,565	2-10-97	9-16-01	4x13"
BB-8	*Alabama*	374'	11,565	12-2-96	10-16-00	4x13"
BB-9	*Wisconsin*	373' 10"	11,653	2-9-97	2-4-01	4x13"
BB-10	*Maine*	393' 11"	12,846	2-15-99	12-29-02	4x12"
BB-11	*Missouri*	393' 11"	12,362	2-7-00	12-1-03	4x12"

Hull No.	Name	Length	Displace-ment	Keel Laid	Commis-sioned	Main Armament
BB-12	Ohio	393' 10"	12,723	4-22-99	10-4-04	4x12"
BB-13	Virginia	441' 3"	14,948	5-21-02	5-7-06	4x12"
BB-14	Nebraska	441' 3"	14,948	7-4-02	7-1-07	4x12"
BB-15	Georgia	441' 3"	14,948	8-31-01	9-24-06	4x12"
BB-16	New Jersey	441' 3"	14,948	4-2-02	5-12-06	4x12"
BB-17	Rhode Island	441' 3"	14,948	5-1-02	2-19-06	4x12"
BB-18	Connecticut	456' 4"	16,000	3-10-03	9-29-06	4x12"
BB-19	Louisiana	456' 4"	16,000	2-7-03	6-2-06	4x12"
BB-20	Vermont	456' 4"	16,000	5-21-04	3-4-07	4x12"
BB-21	Kansas	456' 4"	16,000	2-10-04	4-18-07	4x12"
BB-22	Minnesota	456' 4"	16,000	10-27-03	3-9-07	4x12"
BB-23	Mississippi	382'	13,000	5-12-04	2-1-08	4x12"
BB-24	Idaho	382'	13,000	5-12-04	4-1-08	4x12"
BB-25	New Hampshire	456' 4"	16,000	6-1-05	3-19-08	4x12"
BB-26	South Carolina	452' 9"	16,000	12-18-06	3-1-10	8x12"
BB-27	Michigan	452' 9"	16,000	12-17-06	1-4-10	8x12"
BB-28	Delaware	518' 9"	20,380	11-11-07	4-4-10	10x12"
BB-29	North Dakota	518' 9"	20,000	12-16-07	4-11-10	10x12"
BB-30	Florida	521' 6"	21,825	3-9-09	9-15-11	10x12"
BB-31	Utah	521' 6"	21,825	3-15-19	8-31-11	10x12"
BB-32	Wyoming	562'	20,000	2-9-10	9-25-12	12x12"
BB-33	Arkansas	562'	20,000	1-25-10	9-17-12	12x12"
BB-34	New York	573'	27,000	9-11-11	4-15-14	10x14"
BB-35	Texas	573'	27,000	4-17-11	3-12-14	10x14"
BB-36	Nevada	583'	27,500	11-4-12	3-11-16	10x14"
BB-37	Oklahoma	583'	27,500	10-26-12	5-2-16	10x14"
BB-38	Pennsylvania	608'	31,400	10-27-13	6-12-16	12x14"
BB-39	Arizona	608'	31,400	3-16-14	10-17-16	12x14"
BB-40	New Mexico	624'	32,000	10-14-15	5-20-18	12x14"
BB-41	Mississippi	624'	32,000	4-5-15	12-18-17	12x14"
BB-42	Idaho	624'	32,000	1-20-15	3-24-19	12x14"
BB-43	Tennessee	624' 6"	32,300	5-14-17	6-3-20	12x14"
BB-44	California	624' 6"	32,300	10-25-16	8-10-21	12x14"
BB-45	Colorado	624' 6"	32,600	5-29-19	8-30-23	8x16"
BB-46	Maryland	624' 6"	32,600	4-24-17	7-21-21	8x16"
BB-47	Washington	624' 6"	32,600	6-30-19	(cancelled 2-8-22)	
BB-48	West Virginia	624'	32,600	4-12-20	12-1-23	8x16"
BB-49	South Dakota	624'	32,600	3-15-20	(cancelled 2-8-22)	
BB-50	Indiana	624'	32,600	11-1-20	(cancelled 2-8-22)	
BB-51	Montana	624'	32,600	9-1-20	(cancelled 2-8-22)	
BB-52	North Carolina	624'	32,600	1-12-20	(cancelled 2-8-22)	
BB-53	Iowa	624'	32,600	5-17-20	(cancelled 2-8-22)	
BB-54	Massachusetts	624'	32,600	4-4-21	(cancelled 2-8-22)	
BB-55	North Carolina	728' 9"	35,000	10-27-37	4-9-41	9x16"
BB-56	Washington	729'	35,000	6-14-38	5-15-41	9x16"

Hull No.	Name	Length	Displacement	Keel Laid	Commissioned	Main Armament
BB-57	South Dakota	680'	35,000	7-5-39	3-20-42	9x16"
BB-58	Indiana	680'	35,000	11-20-39	4-30-42	9x16"
BB-59	Massachusetts	680' 10"	35,000	7-20-39	5-12-42	9x16"
BB-60	Alabama	680'	35,000	2-1-40	8-16-42	9x16"
BB-61	Iowa	887' 3"	45,000	6-27-40	2-22-43	9x16"
BB-62	New Jersey	887' 7"	45,000	9-16-40	5-23-43	9x16"
BB-63	Missouri	887' 3"	45,000	1-6-41	6-11-44	9x16"
BB-64	Wisconsin	887' 3"	45,000	1-25-41	4-16-44	9x16"
BB-65	Illinois	887' 3"	45,000	1-15-41	(cancelled 8-12-45)	
BB-66	Kentucky	887' 3"	45,000	12-6-44	(cancelled 2-17-47)	
BB-67	Montana	925'	60,500	(ord.7-19-40 canc. 7-21-43)		
BB-68	Ohio	925'	60,500	(ord. 7-19-40 canc. 7-21-43)		
BB-69	Maine	925'	60,500	(ord. 7-19-40 canc. 7-21-43)		
BB-70	New Hampshire	925'	60,500	(ord. 7-19-40 canc. 7-21-43)		
BB-71	Louisiana	925'	60,500	(ord. 7-19-40 canc. 7-21-43)		

Appendix D

Maryland's Wartime Statistics

Maryland steamed 152,697 miles during World War II.

Ammunition expended:

16-inch 45-caliber main battery	3,479
5-inch 51-caliber secondary battery	6,786
5-inch 25-caliber antiaircraft battery	7,186
40-mm antiaircraft battery	4,093
20-mm antiaircraft battery	10,500

Final armament:

8	16-inch 45-caliber main battery guns
16	5-inch 38-caliber dual purpose secondary battery guns
48	40-mm antiaircraft battery guns
44	20-mm antiaircraft battery guns
116	TOTAL

Her wartime complement was 107 officers, 1,988 enlisted men, and sixty-seven Marines. Of them, fifty-six officers and men were killed in action, sixty-eight were wounded.

BIBLIOGRAPHY

Non-published material

Akagi, Kanji, and Itonaga, Shin, Captain (JMSDF, Ret.) Letter and supporting material, I8 March, 1986, from Mr. Akagi, Professor, Military History Department, The National Institute for Defense Studies, 2 - 2 - 1, Nakameguro - ku, Tokyo, Japan.

Baumrucker., R. O., and Johnson., D. L. *USS* West Virginia *Crosses the Equator Again*, 411 Roosevelt Way, San Francisco, CA, 94114. October., 1944

Crawford, Danny J. *Letter*, History and Museums Division, USMC, Washington, DC, 20380, 5 June, 1985

N. Nav. 37, USS *Maryland*, Roster of Officers, June, 1942.

Pelvin, R. H., Naval Historical Officer, *Letter*, Australian Department of Defense, Navy Office, Russell Offices, Canberra, A.C. T., 2600, Australia, 10 May, 1988.

Reilly, Jr., John C., *Letter*, Ships' Histories Section, Naval Historical Center, Department of the Navy, Washington Navy Yard, Washington, D. C. 20374, 13 September, 1985.

Wiley, H.V. Captain, USN, Commanding Officer, *USS West Virginia, (BB-48) Action in Battle of Surigao Strait 25 October, 1944, USS West Virginia (BB-48) - Report of*, US Naval Historical Center, Washington Navy Yard, Washington, DC, 20374, 1 November, 1944.

Published

Beletat James H. and William M. *Typhoon of Steel, The Battle for Okinawa*. New York, Harper and Row, 1970

Bradley, General Omar N. *A Soldier's Story*, New York, Henry Holt and Company, Inc., 1951

Bryar, Siegfried. *Battleships and Battle Cruisers 1905-1970*, Garden City, N.Y., Doubleday and Company, 1973.

Buell, Thomas B. *The Quiet Warrior, a Biography of Admiral Raymond A. Spruance*, Boston, Little Brown and Company, 1974.

Bulkley, Captain Robert J., Jr., USNR (Retired). *At Close Quarters, PT Boats in the United States Navy*, Washington, D. C., Naval History Division, 1962.

Craig, William. *The Fall of Japan*. New York, The Dial Press, 1967.

Davis, Burke. *Marine! The Life of Chesty Puller*, Boston, Little, Brown & Company, 1962.

Laws, Gavan. *Prisoners of the Japanese*. New York, William Morrow and Company, Inc., 1994.

Dull, Paul S. *A Battle History of the Imperial Japanese Navy (1941-1945)*. Annapolis, Md., Naval Institute Press, 1978.

Fahey, James C. *The Ships and Aircraft of the United States Fleet*, War Edition, 1265 Broadway, New York, Ships and Aircraft, 1942.

Geiger, George John. "Showdown at Jutland." 7950 Deering Ave., Canoga Park, CA., 91304. *Sea Classics*, Vol. 6. No. 4, The Challenge Press, July, 1973.

Gruner, George F. *Blue Water Beat: The Two Lives of the Battleship USS* California. P.O. Box 341, Palo Alto, CA, 94302, The Glencannon Press, 1996.

Hough, Richard. *Dreadnought*. New York, Macmillan Publishing Company, 1964.

Hoyt, Edwin P. *Storm Over the Gilberts, War in the Central Pacific: 1943*. New York, Van Nostrand Reinhold Company, 1978.

---   T*he Battle of Leyte Gulf: The Death Knell of the Japanese Fleet*. New York, Weybright and Talley, 1972.

Inoguehi, Captain Rikihei, and Pineau, Captain Roger, USNR. *The Divine Wind*. Annapolis, Md., Naval Institute Press, 1956

Ito, Masanori, with Pineau, Captain Roger, USNR. *The End of the Imperial Japanese Navy*. New York, W. W. Norton and Company, 1962.

Karig, Commander Walter. *Battle Report, The Atlantic War from the Neutrality Patrol to the Crossing of the Rhine*. New York, Farrar and Rinehart, Inc., 1946.

King, Fleet Admiral Ernest J., USN, and Whitehill, Walter Muir. *Fleet Admiral King, A Naval Record*. New York, W. W. Norton and Company, 1952.

Layton, Rear Admiral Edwin T., USN (Ret.). and Pineau, Captain Roger, USNR, and Costello, John. *"And I Was There," Pearl Harbor and Midway—Breaking the Secrets*. New York, William Morrow and Company, 1985.

Mahan, Captain A. T., USN. *The Influence of Sea Power on History*, New York, Hill Wang, 1957.

Montross Lynn. War Through the Ages. New York, Harper & Brothers, Third Edition. 1960.

Morison, Rear Admiral Samuel Eliot, USNR. *Volume XII, History of United States Naval Operations in World War II*. Boston, Little, Brown and Company, 1958.

---   *The Two Ocean War*. Boston, Atlantic-Little, Brown and Company, 1975.

Orita, Zenji, and Harrington, Joseph D. *I-Boat Captain*. 21335 Roscoe Blvd., Canoga Park, Ca., 91304, Major Books, 1976.

Potter, E. B. *Nimitz*. Annapolis, Md., Naval Institute Press, 1976.

Potter, E. B. and Nimitz, Fleet Admiral Chester W., USN. *The Great Sea War, The Story of Naval Action in World War II*. Englewood Cliffs, N. J., Prentice-Hall, Inc., 1960.

Potter, John Deane. *Yamamoto*. New York, The Viking Press, Inc. 1965.

Prange, Gordon W. *At Dawn We Slept, The Untold Story of Pearl Harbor.* New York, McGraw-Hill Book Company, 1981.

Russ, Martin. *Line of Departure: Tarawa.* Garden City, N.Y., Doubleday & Company, Inc., 1975.

Sakai, Saburo, with Gaidin, Martin, and Saito, Fred. *Samurai!* New York, Bantam Books, Inc., 1978.

Scheer, Admiral. *Germany's High Seas Fleet in the World War.* New York, Peter Smith, 1934.

Smith, Myron J. Jr. *Free State Battlewagon, U.S.S. Maryland (BB-46),* 713 South Third West, Missoula, Mt., 69801, Pictorial Histories Pub. Co., 1986.

Specter., Ronald H. *Eagle Against the Sun, The American War Against Japan.* New York, The Free Press, Macmillan, Inc., 1985.

Toland, John. *Infamy, Pearl Harbor and its Aftermath.* New York, Berkley Publishing Corp., 1983.

Winston, Ensign R.A., USNR. *Dive Bomber,* New York, Holiday House, Inc., 1939.

Authors Unknown

Senshi-Sosho, Kaigun, Shougou Sakusen, Volume 56, (Naval Operations in the Philippine Sea), Asagumo Shimbunsha, Korin Kaikan 3-6--23, Shiba-koen, Minato-Ku. Tokyo, 105, Japan

The Story of the USS Maryland, 1941-1945, Captain J. D. Wilson, USN, commanding, 234 Main Street, Baton Rouge, Louisiana, Army and Navy Pictorial Publishers, 1946.

Index